THE HUMANITY FACTOR

The Humanity Factor

A HEART-DRIVEN APPROACH TO

YOUR FINANCES AND

YOUR FUTURE

FRANK J. LEGAN

LIONCREST
PUBLISHING

THE HUMANITY FACTOR
A Heart-Driven Approach to Your Finances and Your Future

FIRST EDITION

ISBN   978-1-5445-3957-7   *Hardcover*
       978-1-5445-3958-4   *Paperback*
       978-1-5445-3959-1   *Ebook*

To Laura and Reese. You are the standard by which I judge myself and my efforts.

Contents

Introduction

As I'm sitting down to write this book in the pursuit of educating you on my firm's approach to financial planning, I can't help but reflect on one of my clients, whose last day of work is today. Over the years that we've worked together, she's become far more than just a client. She has become family, as many of our clients do. We go through so many different life phases with our clients, and we talk to them so often (and think about their financial future even more often) that it's difficult to think of them as anything other than family.

As I would with a close relative, I'll give her a call tomorrow morning to tell her congratulations and to ask how it feels to be retired. It's so special to us to form these relationships and watch our clients reach the personalized goals they've set for themselves. Watching them succeed never gets old.

Although this client is happily and successfully retiring now, there was certainly a sense of fear in her the first time we spoke. This is something I've seen time and time again in my twenty-three years in this business. When smart people seek out help with their financial affairs, they often walk head-on into a wall of confusion. Most people have no prior knowledge of money management, which means "they don't know what they don't know." They don't know where to start, who to talk to, or what to ask.

More often than not, people who are walking through our door for the first time are scared. Perhaps they have a financial plan that isn't allowing them to hit the goals they want to achieve, or perhaps they don't have a plan at all, and they're nervous to address it. No matter the concern, people are often terrified that they're not going to be OK financially. They want or need reassurance that they'll be alright, and they want to know that their assets and strategies are in alignment with the people and things they care most about in life. So many of them are confused at the onset and want an expert or team of experts—who will play an active role in their future—to walk them through it all in hopes of finding clarity and comfort.

If those feelings of fear heading into this seem familiar to you, let this be your reassurance that you're not alone. Ask yourself an important question right now: do I believe my future is bigger than my past? I hope your answer is yes, because it absolutely is, especially when using our unique approach to planning.

THE ORIGIN OF THE HUMANITY FACTOR™

My firm, Cedar Brook Group, was founded back in 2005 with a mission of helping people eliminate their fears regarding money, get clear on what they want for their future, and realize their goals. We often have to remind our clients that sometimes things get worse before they get better, but going through the process may work out if they're dedicated to learning, applying, and trusting our approach.

Here's what's wrong with many other approaches to planning: the financial industry has convinced people that planning is about numbers, first and foremost. My twenty years of professional experience has formed my opinion that a humanity-driven approach to financial planning helps clients reach their financial goals more effectively than a market-driven approach.

We, on the other hand, look at things differently. Instead of being just numbers-centric—resulting in hollow conversations with clients, ones that lack any grounding in what really makes sense for that individual—we aim to be people-centric instead. Our approach bypasses stoic traditions and starts with what matters: the people and things in life that you care about most. Because of its human-focused nature, we call it The Humanity Factor™. We've been successfully using it for over two decades, and our clients have benefited from it.

This book will offer a step-by-step guide to The Humanity Factor, providing you with a thorough understanding of the approach, as well as tools and lessons you can apply on your own to build your personalized financial plan and do so with confidence. If you don't necessarily know where you want to be right now, fear not, as this book will get you there. And if finance seems like a foreign language to you, this book will help you begin to speak it fluently because there is a high cost that comes with not learning the language. This book will teach you the language in a way that makes sense because it grounds the conversation in the important things: your loved ones and how you spend your time.

You'll notice The Humanity Factor asks you to be vulnerable and honest about your fears and insecurities in order to come away with the best plan for your nest egg and a new perspective on who you are and what you want out of life. To help you define and pursue your future, we'll dive into your past: your challenges and triumphs, the role you play in your community, your family history, and your aspirations. Only then can you prudently and powerfully decide where to go.

A PEOPLE-FIRST APPROACH

So, why not a numbers-first approach to planning? Well, I can confidently say that, in my opinion, a humanity-driven approach leads to far more successful outcomes than a typical numbers-centric approach. We've learned this firsthand at Cedar Brook through interactions with clients about their overall happiness and satisfaction level. Clients have told us time and time again that this approach makes them feel far more confident as well. They've also shown more patience and understanding using this approach when times get tough because they have heightened certainty that their plan is right for *them*—instead of created in some vacuum—and that they have a greater chance of success. Because their plan through The Humanity Factor is one that is directly aligned with the things that are most important to them, they feel more excited about it, too.

With a numbers-first approach, clients have interactions with their advisors that tend to be mind-numbing—staring at numbers on a paper and comparing how they're doing to some sort of numerical benchmark. On the flip side, even in difficult times, humanity-driven conversations are based on gratitude as the foundation, as you'll come to learn. This is why we developed a *different* kind of benchmark, The Experience Index™, which we'll discuss in Chapter 7. These conversations make people feel good because they're talking about the things that are personal to them and the things that bring them joy.

On our end, we use The Humanity Factor to ensure our clients know we have a shared purpose and that we're truly working on their behalf.[1] We thoroughly enjoy getting people to where they want to go, and we see it as an honor to be invited on their journey. We find it exciting and rewarding, and it makes for meetings in which everyone feels enthusiastic.

Once you begin applying The Humanity Factor, you'll quickly find that you're asking, *"Will I be OK?"* far less often. It will help you realize that you are on track and your dreams are within reach. For those that are off track, we can help adjust their plans and course-correct. It will also help you move away from any traditional thinking about finances that cause unnecessary comparisons to the people around you. You don't have to keep up with the Joneses! Instead, you'll focus on achieving a life that matters to you.

WHEN IT COMES TO MONEY, SIMPLICITY IS BEAUTIFUL

Simplicity is a beautiful thing, and that's something else I love about The Humanity Factor—it's straightforward as could be. Other planners may make their approach complicated because

---

1   Second Summer home page, accessed December 8, 2022, https://secondsummer.net/.

they want you to need them. From where we're sitting, our job is to make the complex simple.

People who come to us are confused about the language on its own, and we don't want them to feel even more overwhelmed. When we remove the concern about the numbers, we're able to whittle it down to what matters most and continue putting that at the center of all we do. The Humanity Factor helps get to the *what* and *why* behind a person's plan.

We want to know why a person has been driven to get out of bed every morning and go to work every day for forty years, giving it their best every day. We want to know what it was all about. What was it for? The simplicity of defining that is beautiful.

Our goal is to disrupt their expectations in a nice way. We make it a point to walk people through the fine print, but we realize they don't need to know all of the ins and outs that we do as advisors. So, we keep it relevant to them and prevent them from having to get into the weeds. Then, we use our knowledge to take their plan to the next level and get them where they want to go.

The Humanity Factor encourages you to leave the numbers to the experts. We're in the field for a reason, after all. Personally, I always had an interest in financial planning and enjoyed the concepts of being responsible with money and investing. If I had free time, I would read about financial planning and investing, how to do more with less, and how to maximize what you have. When I was in graduate school, I interned with my parents' financial advisor and fell in love with the business from my first day on the job. I liked the idea of having the resources to do the things I wanted to. I wanted to live a life that was very comfortable financially and strived not to work paycheck to paycheck. Pursuing a career as an advisor became the perfect path for me.

DOING IT DIFFERENTLY

When looking for a firm, I knew I didn't just want to work at a place that was simply transactional. I saw early on how important the human element was to creating and executing the best financial plan possible for people. I noticed how many people in our field got caught up in the numbers and did so to a fault. I also saw how many people were living each day with the goal of simply outdoing their colleagues, neighbors, or other family members financially. People everywhere seemed to be losing sight of what they wanted for their own financial future because they were too busy paying attention to someone else.

I wanted to work somewhere where being the biggest revenue generator wasn't the main concern but instead was more focused on doing *good* for clients. Many advisors can analyze a spreadsheet, but can you have a meaningful conversation with them? Or get a hug from them afterward, as if they were a member of your family? Having a human connection makes clients more appreciative of the work being done for—and with—them.

When I found Cedar Brook, I knew it was the place I'd envisioned working. I saw how the advisors here were really delving into clients' strengths, values, and dreams to create a meaningful fiscal plan for their future. Cedar Brook was founded on creating a place for clients and advisors to collaborate, which simply didn't exist in the marketplace. They decided to create it themselves.

Cedar Brook was started by a group of guys who worked for a national financial services firm here in Cleveland, Ohio. There was a leadership change that happened, and they all quickly realized, from a value standpoint, that the organization changed drastically. They'd all been happy prior to that change in leadership, but afterward, they looked around and didn't feel like it suited them anymore. They decided to start their own firm with their vision of how things should be: they wanted to keep *people*, not numbers, at the forefront.

I've been with Cedar Brook for over a decade now, and from the moment that I walked through the front door, I knew this was home. It's a place where you come because you want to be a part of something that's bigger than yourself, and that's just what has happened to me. To say I'm proud of the team we've built at Cedar Brook would be an understatement. We're admittedly obsessed with our culture of putting our clients above anything else, and maintaining that culture is the #1 most important thing to us. It's a really special place because of it. Not only are our clients like family, but our entire team at Cedar Brook is like family, too. We take collaboration to the next level because we know that to most effectively get our clients where they want to go, shared knowledge amongst us internally is so very vital.

I feel lucky to be surrounded by such good people at Cedar Brook, from my colleagues to the families we work with. Not only do we have the same values, but we also have the same kind of spirit of wanting to serve others. Contemplation and creativity are alive and well in between meetings with clients— meaning that they trust us and give us permission to brainstorm and innovate on their behalf. It's more of a partnership than anything else.

When I look around internally, I see advisors who really care. I would trust them one hundred times over with my own financial goals—to make sure my wife and daughter would be taken care of in the event anything happened to me, to make investments that are driven around those things, and to make sure that estate planning strategies (both investment-wise and tax-wise) are all aligned as such. I know my family would be cared for. I couldn't say that about anywhere else I've worked.

A TRIED AND TRUE METHOD

By using The Humanity Factor, we've learned a lot about who our clients are as individuals, parents, leaders, mentors, creatives, philanthropists, and so on. Throughout this book, I'll give examples of how this approach has worked for some of them. While the examples in the book are all based on real experiences, the names have been changed for privacy purposes. What you'll easily pick up from the examples is just how effective this approach can be and how much confidence it can bring.

I want to note up front here that this is not a book about quickly getting the highest return. In fact, we find that short-term solutions often lead to long-term problems. So if you're focused only on the numbers, you're in the wrong place. Instead, this book will teach you how to remain focused on the things you want for your financial future.

Going through The Humanity Factor helps people reflect on themselves. And, as I've mentioned, clients benefit from it greatly. We've actually seen that while focusing on the "why" of it all rather than the numbers, clients actually earn a much better rate of return using this approach, and they challenge themselves to dream bigger for their futures than they would have otherwise. They learn to realize their strengths, be grateful, and give themselves credit where credit is due.

YOUR TICKET TO A GREAT ADVISOR AND A BRILLIANT PLAN

Our approach—one that's worked many times—may work for you too. You can apply The Humanity Factor to yourself as an individual, to your family, and/or to your business. I recommend that if you don't already have an advisor who follows a similar approach, seek one who does. The ideal advisor will be one who has integrity and has your best interest at heart. The kind of advisor you should be looking for is one who cares about you and the things you care about. You should work with someone or a team of people who are grateful to be helping you.

How can you tell if the advisor follows a humanity-centric approach? It will be apparent through the questions they ask and whether the advisor is talking more than they're listening. If the advisor is someone who leads with their capabilities in order to tell you how smart and amazing they are, they probably aren't the type of advisor I'm recommending here. It shouldn't be about them, or about me as an advisor, or about Cedar Brook advisors, or anyone else. This process should be about you.

At Cedar Brook, our clients have become so comfortable sharing things with us, and that's how it should be. We're then able to celebrate their wins with candor and kindness. Being vulnerable and open can be a stretch for some people, but remember, as you're going through this process, how positively it will affect you down the road if you're able to show that vulnerability.

Whether you're currently in the best of times or the worst of times when it comes to your finances, The Humanity Factor will help you look toward the best future possible and provide a roadmap to help you achieve it. Again, if you're anxious or nervous going into this, that's normal! Think of it this way: no matter your current situation, someone has definitely been there before and has gotten out of it. You've got this.

Building and protecting a nest egg should not have to be an uphill battle. My hope is that success can be yours and The Humanity Factor may help you attain it. Using The Humanity Factor, I believe it can be.

Best of luck in personalizing your financial plan!

—FRANK J. LEGAN

CHAPTER 1

The Humanity Factor™

All financial plans are not created equal.

That statement should be fairly apparent, but for many clients, it's not—they simply don't see it that way. When it comes to managing money, people tend to follow conventional wisdom, putting themselves in a one-size-fits-all category with others of varying financial and personal circumstances and goals. The truth is, listening to the conventional wisdom on this topic is corrosive; following it can wear away at your financial— and often, mental—well-being. This is because conventional wisdom tells us to focus primarily on the numbers but says very little about the person behind the money and why they're saving. Conventional wisdom tends to disregard a person's unique story.

Part of the problem is that—somewhere along the line—we've been trained to compare ourselves to the Joneses. As a result, we tend to dwell on what others have—maybe it's our neighbors, relatives, or friends who we believe have more money than we do. We stay up at night wondering how we can get where they are and what they have and achieve their perceived level of financial freedom. We want to follow their exact path because it's worked for them, at least as far as we know. But after many years in the financial planning business, I'll confidently tell you something upfront about this way of thinking (and living, for that matter). It will only set you back.

No matter who you are, what you do, or your current financial standing, your finances and your financial plan are always, and I repeat *always,* unique to you. Numbers only tell part of a person's financial story, no matter how big or small those numbers are. You cannot simply follow the exact plan someone else used based on numbers alone and expect it to work precisely the same for you.

Theodore Roosevelt once famously said, "Comparison is the thief of joy." I can't count the times I've witnessed this notion come to life in my business. Someone will walk into Cedar Brook, and they'll start describing an ultra-rich friend of theirs, or someone they know with far less debt, or someone who has gotten huge returns on high-risk investments, and they'll say, "I want what they have." Unfortunately, they can't see this tendency robbing them of their financial happiness. They're so stuck mentally on someone else's wealth and how to apply it to their life that they can't wrap their head around their own wealth. In some cases, they may even be in better financial standing than the person they're comparing themselves to; they just don't realize it.

I'll tell clients to stop and refocus when these conversations present themselves. Comparing their financial situation with someone else's not only steals their joy but is also a completely pointless exercise.

REPLACE COMPARISON WITH PURPOSE

Right now, you may know of someone with a large nest egg, but if their expenses are high, they will need a lot more to make their life work when they retire. On the flip side, you may be someone with a low spend and guaranteed income and pension, like a teacher or a paramedic. As a result, your nest egg won't have to be nearly as big as the other person, even though you perceive them to have more numbers on the scoreboard right now.

No matter how you slice it, comparing where you're at financially with others—paying too much attention to what anyone else has or what they're doing—is never a good idea. Our first order of business is getting you to omit that way of thinking. It's step one to finding financial success with our company's approach to financial planning.

People who constantly compare themselves to others tend to be focused only on numbers. Yes, Cedar Brook cares about numbers, but we know financial planning is only partly a numbers game. More importantly, planning for your future should be about determining *your story*—one that is undoubtedly unique and using it to develop a financial plan that's right for you and your family. People have different goals. For some, the most important thing right now is buying a new house. For others, the priority is financial flexibility. We want to get you where you want to be money-wise while also focusing on who you are as an individual. Because our approach was developed with *you* in mind, humanizing the financial planning process, we call it The Humanity Factor.

Humanity is the quality of kindness, of being human. A *factor* is one who actively contributes to an accomplishment or result.

The Humanity Factor™ is our belief that by honoring you as the central figure in your own planning, you may achieve unprecedented results.

That personal component is part of the process many financial planners neglect. I get it: I'm a numbers guy too, so in our world, it can be difficult to put numbers on the back burner, but we need to be realistic: there is a human element behind developing and executing the best financial plan. If we don't consider the "you" factor, we're just throwing your plan into a cookie-cutter model. In the best-case scenario, the cookie-cutter plan works out alright. But in the worst case, it can lead to major financial losses and a pit-in-your-stomach feeling of emptiness, a sense that you're spending your whole life going through the motions.

I've said it once, and I'll repeat it: Everyone has a unique financial situation, no matter who they are. Even in the case of two business partners who make the same amount annually, they'll need to have unique plans depending on various factors, like the size of their family, their monthly budget, their health, and their values, just to name a few. Plus, at the very core, despite potential financial similarities between people, everyone has different things that drive them to save. That "why" makes us all unique if nothing else.

This book sets out to help you develop the right plan for you with all of this in mind. First, I will guide you through The Humanity Factor, the approach we use with every client who walks through our door. The Humanity Factor will give you a tailored approach to managing your money. Then, I'll give you all of the lessons and tools you'll need so you can apply The Humanity Factor to come up with your own plan.

THE ORIGIN OF THE HUMANITY FACTOR

Before we go any further, let's quickly talk about how The Humanity Factor came to be. Years ago, we realized that if you ask a dozen financial advisors what they do, they would likely answer the same way we were answering this question at Cedar Brook: "We do financial planning, wealth preservation, and investment management."

Yes, we were classically trained like the others, meaning we were good at math, understood the investing world and tax and estate planning strategies, and knew how to maximize opportunities and long-term market trends. We knew how to help people navigate life through numbers. In addition, we had continuing education opportunities to stay sharp at our jobs. So, on the surface, we all looked alike.

But while their services and training looked the same as ours, we knew our work was nothing like the others in our industry. Anybody can chase returns or give technical advice; with some financial advisors, their entire value proposition was "I'm better at investing than everybody else." But all financial advisors work on a level playing field regarding the numbers; the rules around retirement plans, taxes, and estate planning are the same for every individual and every firm. So what actually matters is the questions your advisor is asking you.

The Humanity Factor became a way to describe our approach and the value we were bringing to the lives of our clients. For us, it was—and continues to be—about great relationships built on a mutual desire to learn, grow, and better ourselves. We call that Cultivating our Contributions. Our clients' wins are our wins, and their losses are our losses. That's the heart and soul of who we are at Cedar Brook.

The Humanity Factor is a behavior pattern that existed before we named it. We knew we were different, we just didn't know how to say it. We wanted to be clear about the business model and the nature of our client-partner relationships, so we needed a new way to describe what we do.

That's when we rolled out The Humanity Factor™ to our existing clients. After the launch, we checked in with them and asked, "Is this reminiscent of your experience with us?" Because if it wasn't, our clients would call us out. The client and planner relationship is intimate, and clients tell you personal things: their finances, insecurities, and fears, but also their hopes and dreams. They might not even share those things with their families at Thanksgiving dinner, but they share them with us. So, our clients would tell us if we weren't treating them with humanity, compassion, and care.

BREAKING THE MOLD

People who have had a bad experience with their financial advisor come into Cedar Brook and may already be skeptical. They can be hesitant, confused, and mistrusting. They can be on the verge of being done with the financial services industry. So for those clients, a different approach resonates.

Additionally, clients deserve to go somewhere they won't feel embarrassed. People come to me, hat in hand, and ask, "Hey, is what I have in my bank account even good?" I can tell they've been steered in the wrong direction by corrosive conventional wisdom. They come into my office terrified: "I read an article that said by my age, people have X saved. I don't have that. Am I going to be alright?"

My answer is, "Okay. X sure is an interesting number to try and hit, but why? What are you trying to achieve? Who are you saving for?" There's no context. That's why we made it our mission to ask those clarifying questions. Figuring out what makes each client tick helps us create a financial plan that boasts relevant returns while meeting their unique goals. So, The Humanity Factor became our way of explaining how our approach differs from the rest.

Most people in our industry help their clients save for the future by solely focusing on the numbers. Clients tell them, on a surface level, where they hope their finances will be at retirement, and they collectively build a plan around that. Unfortunately, that discovery conversation—and all of their subsequent conversations—become about the numbers and the numbers alone. These clients search for clarity and confidence and instead find themselves more confused. Their advisor may crunch the numbers and toss them back with little explanation and no personal meaning behind them. It can leave clients feeling empty and lost.

From where we're sitting, that's not enough. We know if we're not taking the time to understand the motivation behind why people are saving, then we're missing the whole point.

YOUR PURPOSE IS THE FOUNDATION OF YOUR PLAN

Not only are number-centered conversations hollow, but they also make the process of saving for your future downright dull. Without your eyes set on your purpose, you're going into your nine-to-five every day for forty years, saying, "I just have to get to this age, with this amount of money saved, and then I'll be set." It can become a grueling way of viewing things. You're essentially just trudging through life. The way I see it, it's not a meaningful existence.

As I walk you through The Humanity Factor, we will—of course—get to the numbers, but first, we need to understand who you are as a human being. We consider this process the development of your unique story. We'll take a holistic and calm approach to planning.

We want to know what makes you "you." To do this, we must consider the people and things that matter. We want to know about your role in your family and your career, your relationships, and what else is important to you, like philanthropy or mentorship. We want to know what things bring you joy. We not only *want* to know these things, but we also *need* to know them. We need to understand your whole picture so we can determine what strategies will work best for your situation.

Following The Humanity Factor will encourage you to participate in your financial plan actively. Here are some questions to start considering:

- Who am I as a human being? (A wife, mother, father, husband, partner, engineer, artist, or business owner?)
- What are the challenges in my life?
- What is my primary driver for saving?
- What really matters to me?
- Who do I care most about?
- What role do I play for others financially?
- What is my family history?
- What are my aspirations for the future?

Having these honest conversations with yourself will help you move away from that conventional wisdom and a mentality of comparing yourself. Answering these types of questions will help you get to the core of why saving is important to you. Is it because you want to ensure your spouse will always be cared for? Is it vital that you leave your children a certain amount of money when your time comes? Developing your unique story will help determine what you're motivated by, what your passions are, and what your purpose is. What is your "why"?

A CARING APPROACH CREATES IMPACTFUL OUTCOMES

You'll need to commit to this process by asking yourself honest questions. At Cedar Brook, when we do this exercise with clients 1:1, we leave the conversation open-ended so that our clients consider what is important to them on an ongoing basis, realizing things are constantly changing. We tell them that if they aren't willing to have these conversations, then The Humanity Factor is likely not the right fit for them.

We've been using The Humanity Factor for nearly two decades, and we've seen it work repeatedly. People come to us because we are committed to operating in Shared Purpose, as opposed to being with an advisor who uses planning as a tool to sell products. Instead, we become like family.

Shared Purpose® taught us that, as an advisory firm, we do our best work based on the quality of our relationships and environment. Shared Purpose isn't just about how we plan, it's also a way of describing *who* we work best with. Working with clients who are a good fit for our company culture and who share our values and ideals protects our client service model.

I have one client, Darryl, a retired firefighter/paramedic who now works as a bus driver for a local school in his community. His pension covers more than his expenses, but Darryl is a saver. He's saved throughout his life to ensure his wife and daughter are cared for when he's gone. His daughter is now married, and she and her husband are financially stable, with two kids. However, Darryl has never turned off the thought that he needs to provide and care for her. He was happy, but he knew there were many more fun things he could be doing with his money; he just wasn't sure he had enough expendable cash to meet all of his goals.

But he did. Using The Humanity Factor, we got very clear on Darryl's "why." Once we learned what mattered to him, we crunched the numbers. We found that Darryl could continue saving for what was important *and* find time to pursue his retirement dreams, such as visiting Disney with his grandkids. He regularly tells me that he loves working with Cedar Brook because we make him feel like family. *That's* The Humanity Factor.

We care deeply about the impact this approach makes. Anyone can be productive in this business, but to be impactful is something else altogether. That's the good stuff. Of course, we all want to make a good living and provide for our families, but to make an impact on people's lives just by getting them to think differently about financial planning is where the magic is made.

Applying The Humanity Factor in situations like Darryl's, we get to see how it provides confidence for people. It lessened his stress about dollars, encouraged him to do the things he loves, and brought confidence and clarity around his present and future.

As we continue to bring new clients on board with The Humanity Factor, we work with them 1:1 as a team. This means we're internally bouncing ideas and best practices off each other and bringing in outside experts to help us lead our clients into the future. We do this so that we're not just using one person's worldview to guide the approach. Instead, we have others weigh in with different perspectives and tactics. These tactics help The Humanity Factor evolve while helping to improve our clients' best outcomes.

FEAR IS NORMAL IN THE MIDST OF CHANGE

Before we dive into creating your unique story in the next chapter, I want to offer another bit of advice upfront for those nervous about this process. I often tell my clients that things may get worse before they get better. That feeling creeps in when you're unsure of the process of financial planning as a whole—because of that, even picking up this book may have caused some initial hesitation on your end. The process can be intimidating, especially if you don't know much about the topic. But don't be scared. We'll alleviate that fear by going through the exact steps you need to follow and doing so in an easy-to-understand manner.

Your numbers may be causing you some fear as well. But again, don't be scared. We're here to walk you through the process. Things may have to get worse before they get better, but they can get better. You just have to commit to doing the work. If your numbers are something you've been avoiding, or if they're something you don't like to address because you're embarrassed or fearful, we still need to address it. Following the actions and questions in this book will ensure you're no longer turning a blind eye.

If you've made some financial mistakes in the past, don't beat yourself up over it. We can help clean it up. I like to say that everyone has a history and a future. We've all had life experiences: things we've done that we're proud of and things that haven't gone right, and it all brings us to where we are today and makes us grateful for what we have. Our history drives the decisions we make in life. So use that history to get eager about your future—because it can be anything you want it to be.

We want people to be grateful and to have a mindset that their future is bigger than their past. By understanding your wins and losses, your current strengths, and your individual needs, we can help get you to a better place. Whether you're in excellent financial standing or on shaky ground, remember that someone out there has been in your shoes before and has still created a successful financial plan. (But your plan, of course, will be uniquely tailored to you.)

I've often found that most people don't give themselves enough credit. They don't think they have enough money to get started, or they've made too many financial mistakes already. But it's simply not true. No matter where you're starting, it's the commitment *to* start that matters.

Getting too caught up in past financial mistakes can send someone into a tailspin. For example, consider two of our clients, a married couple, Harold and Lydia. Harold was a very successful businessman who invented a type of technology decades ago that made him a great fortune. With money at their fingertips, the couple was introduced to an advisor with a history of good returns who worked in a niche of high-yielding investments.

Harold and Lydia didn't realize that higher yield can mean higher risk. The markets began getting away from them, and their losses started mounting. Seeing their statements, they became very concerned. They wanted to know what was happening and how to stop the bleeding. Because their plan with their advisor had been all about the numbers—targeting a high number return with no personal conversation about their past, present, or future motivators—they were at a loss.

They knew they needed a change of tactic, so their accountant introduced them to us, and we began developing a plan to get them back on track. Harold is ninety-five years old now and slowing down, so Lydia—who is about fifteen years younger—became the CFO of the family so that her husband wouldn't have to spend his last years poring over financial statements and expenses. Lydia was tenacious and smart in the CFO role, and though she was not overly familiar with the numbers, she knew their finances were in turmoil. As a result, Lydia panicked, and rightfully so. We calmed her down with The Humanity Factor, getting to the core of *why* they wanted savings built up: so that she and their children and grandchildren were taken care of.

Knowing their specific goals, we recommended against riskier investments like the ones they'd been previously invested in because, though those had a chance of a bigger return, the risk was too high. We talked about transforming her dangers and maximizing her opportunities. The danger was that the market could have spoiled their retirement. We solved that by having a more conservative allocation because the amount of risk they had been taking did not match Lydia's more risk-averse personality.

Lydia was fearful they were spending more than could be sustained, but that wasn't true. We reviewed their numbers and proved to Lydia that they had plenty of money to live the rest of their lives as they wanted. Their previous financial advisor had regularly talked over her head and spit numbers and jargon at her, all in a condescending tone, so Lydia had been intimidated. This is enough to scare anyone who doesn't fully understand the numbers. He might as well have been speaking to her in another language. Through the lens of The Humanity Factor, Lydia was able to understand the numbers more clearly.

This approach helped Lydia get out of the "I've got to earn the best return" rat race and instead gave her confidence in their financial strategy based on their values and goals. Lydia went from being nervous and unable to sleep, thinking their financial life was crumbling away, to becoming a calmer and happier version of herself. That shift happened when we started making this plan about the things they cared about—their children and grandchildren, their pride and joy—and doing so in a simplistic way that Lydia could more clearly wrap her head around. Then, and only then, was there that sense of relief.

If our planning were only about the numbers without the context, it would have caused more anxiety, hollowness, and lack of meaning. Now, they have perspective; they can see the bigger picture. Lydia and I talk regularly, and she can ask me questions whenever she wants. When she does, I'm sure to explain things to her clearly and without jargon.

So, how do you start to move your mind from, "I want to keep up with those around me," or—in the case of Harold and Lydia in the past, "let's aim for the biggest numbers possible"—to "let's make a plan that *matters* to me"? The answer is simple: Apply The Humanity Factor.

YOUR BIGGER FUTURE IS WAITING

If you're ready and willing, now is the time to set yourself up for a stress-free future. Are you prepared to change your perception of financial planning and how you can look at your future? If you've been worried about achieving the numbers so you can retire, now you're going to think about your financial plan differently. This book aims to align those numbers with your goals, values, and dreams.

It's time to leave your frustration behind and get excited about your financial future. You can breathe a sigh of relief as you break free of the corrosive conventional wisdom. Trust that you can come up with the right plan for you and meet your savings and retirement goals—you just need to be clear about what those are, with the "why" front and center.

It's time to get specific to you. What is your unique story? What are your dreams? Why are you planning for the future? We'll need that story to guide you in building a meaningful financial plan.

Let's get into it.

CHAPTER 2

Your Unique Story

By now, you should have a solid understanding of The Humanity Factor and how it differs from other numbers-only financial planning approaches. Importantly, lots of advisory relationships include great questions and deep discussions. We believe it's crucial to look at the motivation behind those questions—and what the advisors do with the answers.

With that grounding, it's time to start developing a plan unique to you. We'll begin the process by getting you into the right mindset, which is a critical but overlooked part of planning. With a negative mindset, achieving even the simplest goals can be difficult. With a positive mindset, the world is yours.

To get your thoughts flowing in a positive direction, we'll start to consider you and your background, taking stock of all the things you bring to your plan. Because, no matter who you are, you have *a lot* to bring to the table—whether you believe that or not.

MEASURING BACKWARD TO FOSTER POSITIVITY

When it comes to finances, one of the worst things you can do is measure yourself against a future, "ideal" version of yourself. Clients often come to us with their minds bogged down by a vision of who they would be *if only* their financial future were perfect and *if only* they hadn't made mistakes in the past. They'll beat themselves up until it's all they think about. Striving for perfection prevents you from seeing everything you've accomplished so far.

If the above sounds like you, stop beating yourself up. This way of thinking will always lead to frustration and disappointment because the "ideal" version of your finances is unobtainable. So, instead of focusing on a *perfect* financial future, we encourage our clients to "measure backward." Measuring backward is a crucial part of Mining Your Bliss, which you'll learn about later in this chapter. I wanted to share the concept with you early on because it's a great way to establish your mindset when reading the chapter *and* the book.

So then, what, exactly, is measuring backward?[2] Measuring backward asks you to look closely at your background, dive into your past successes, and account for the strengths and resources you can draw on now. This practice encourages you to be grateful for past accomplishments, no matter how big or small, and use those to foster ongoing positivity about your financial standing. And measuring backward now will train you to be grateful for the accomplishments you have coming your way.

---

2   Dan Sullivan and Benjamin Hardy, *The Gap and The Gain: The High Achievers' Guide to Happiness, Confidence, and Success* (Carlsbad, CA: Hay House Business, 2021).

Start by asking yourself:

- What financial wins have I been most proud of in my life so far?
- What are my biggest strengths when it comes to money?
- What seeds have I planted that will bear fruit in the future?
- What foundations have I laid that I can build upon?

People don't give themselves credit for even the simplest things, like having good money habits, not spending more than they make, and being good stewards of their family's resources. The truth is, those things are a big deal. But unfortunately, sometimes, people don't recognize their wins and how they can capitalize on them.

Another overlooked win is being good at your job. Because a person's Unique Ability® comes naturally, they may not give themselves credit. It's important to stop and consider everything that's helping you financially, even if it seems to come easily.[3] We find that becoming clear and present about your sources of pride and passion naturally stimulates your best thinking.

One more thing we like to encourage at Cedar Brook is celebrating milestones. Consider the evolution of a married couple, Sam and Deborah, who set out on a winding path to retirement, including job changes, children, and so on. They dreamt big along the way but celebrated their wins at every chance. They'd sit down with a glass of wine and toast, "Wow, we did this," every time they hit a milestone in their plan. That's what

---

3   Strategic Coach home page, accessed December 8, 2022, https://www.strategiccoach.com/.

it's about—being proud of the goals you met instead of being fixated on the idea of, "That's great, but if we only had more…".

People put too much pressure on themselves to get that second home or higher-paying job, which brings them stress and negativity. Instead, you should focus on all that you've already accomplished, where you've made it in life, and be proud of it. That very act of measuring backward brings about more fulfillment and optimism.

Often, people are so busy hard-charging toward the future that they don't take time to think back on how far they've come. Focusing on today has become a lost art. If you look back instead of forward and say, "How am I different today than I was six years ago?" you'll find progress, often significant progress. This process is about being present and taking stock of yourself and what you have to bring to the table.

If you've taken the initiative to pick up this book, I bet you're also someone who gets up every day and gives it their best. In addition, you likely have goals and are working toward achieving them. Over time, all of that effort compounds and yields positive outcomes.

One of my clients, Molly, is someone who tends to be too hard on herself. She is an accountant, so she's all about the numbers and loves her spreadsheets. Molly worked as a banker in Cleveland when she realized she wanted to become a CPA and eventually move to Southern California with her husband.

But Molly was fixated on repaying her student loan debt before she moved out west. During a planning meeting, she expressed frustration that she wasn't further along in that goal. The fact is, she had already made a huge dent in it. I told her, "Look, you're measuring wrong." I pointed out that she had a lot of valuable skills and career experience. I explained that she and her husband were actually well situated to make a move, and together, we measured backward to prove it.

Feeling more confident, Molly and her husband took the plunge, and it paid off. She got a great job at an accounting firm in Los Angeles, and they quickly made a life for themselves. Recently, Molly made partner at her CPA firm, and they bought a house. By all accounts, they're doing it right. But at the end of the day, Molly is still a numbers girl and still worries about paying off her college loan debt. And that's OK because I continue to take her through the process of measuring backward—and now she has even *more* to show for herself.

There are so many accomplishments for you to feel good about. It's all about your mindset, so take a moment and consider how far you've come: *measure backward*.

On your way there? Good!

ESTABLISHING YOUR UNIQUE STORY

Now that your mind is on the right track, let's get into your Unique Story. As we covered in Chapter 1, the Unique Story conversation helps diagnose who you are, what you've done, and where you are now in order to plan what's next. In addition, it enables you to gain awareness of your unique situation.

At Cedar Brook, we find that awareness alleviates frustration.

Time and again, we find that bringing awareness to what's going well in the client's life can help calm their frustrations and concerns. This process tends to leave clients feeling good about the future because it gives them clarity on what they value now and how to preserve and expand upon those cherished values in the future. If you tend to be focused on the numbers, just remember that toiling over spreadsheets can only bring you so much clarity.

Defining your unique story will communicate the most vital things about you to your advisor. Only then can you get the powerful, poignant solutions you're seeking. The purpose of developing your Unique Story is similar to why you'd visit a doctor for a diagnosis. You must be honest and open with them to get the best diagnosis and create the best healthcare plan. We'll apply the same logic here.

There are three elements we use to fully define your Unique Story as part of The Humanity Factor. The first we call **Mine Your Bliss**, and it's focused on your past. The second we call **Cultivate Your Contributions**, and it's focused on your present. The third is called **The Leadership Lever,** which focuses on your future. These elements will help you understand your "why" now and into the future.

MINE YOUR BLISS

Mine Your Bliss calls on you to dive deep into your past to understand what drives you. Mining Your Bliss helps you take stock of what you did yesterday and teaches you how to capitalize on your achievements. In addition, this practice helps you identify your strengths, which you can leverage into opportunities.

You've already done the first and most important step in Mining Your Bliss—measuring backward. Now you'll start asking yourself, "What enlivens me *now*? What are my present-day strengths and successes?" Mining Your Bliss uncovers a lot about you and keeps your mind focused on the right things.

We believe in Mining Your Bliss because it helps you get clear on what your sources of pride and passion are. It also gets you grounded so that you can think about your biggest dreams and aspirations for the future. This newfound clarity will fuel the right thinking about what you want for *your* future instead of focusing on the "ideal" version of your future self and feeling like you're behind where you want to be.

You might wonder, "As a financial company and wealth advisor, how do you get your clients to take this kind of personal journey with you?" The answer is simple: we ask a few thoughtful questions to get them to a place of gratitude:

- What am I most proud of in my life?
- What accomplishments mean the most to me?
- What am I grateful for?
- What makes me excited?
- How has my family impacted my way of thinking about finances?
- What other relationships have impacted my way of thinking about finances?

Family is usually an area of focus here, as for many people, their family is central to their lives (and their financial plans). There are two sides to every family's history: the challenges and the triumphs. Like most things, much of it will depend on your mindset when considering family history.

Relationships play a part here, too. The importance of relationships is that they're a strength—they're what gets you out of the weeds and focused on the things that are of the most value to people. They're what people cherish the most because financial resources are for the people in their life that they love. It's something that they want to share. Most people aren't just in it for themselves. It's about sharing with spouses, children, grandchildren, siblings, and friends. It's also about creating a shared purpose community around you that will support you in building the brightest, most secure future.

Here is an example of how my family tackled Mining Our Bliss. Shortly after my daughter, Reese, was born, my wife Laura was diagnosed with Multiple Sclerosis. After we left the doctor's office, our heads were spinning. Left alone with our own thoughts, we ruminated over worst-case scenarios and dark possibilities. Would Laura be able to walk for the rest of her life? Was I going to become her full-time caregiver? These thoughts plagued us for weeks, but we eventually realized we needed to center ourselves—for our daughter and us. It would've been easy to keep going down a rabbit hole, thinking about what life might look like in the future. Instead, we decided to focus on what we *did* have—we took stock of everything, including all that we'd been through together and how much we'd accomplished so far in life. The fact we had each other was our most valuable resource.

Although the game changed for us with this diagnosis, we looked at it through this lens: Every day is a gift. We didn't know what tomorrow would bring, so it forced us to be more present and not put things off. It pushed us to take the trips we wanted, have the experiences we dreamed about, and not waste a single day we had with our daughter.

During the pandemic, Laura was then also diagnosed with Lupus. Again, we could have let this drag us into a constant state of worry, but instead, we chose to Mine Our Bliss. In doing so, we reignited our gratitude and focused on treating every day like a gift. We've accelerated our winter-optional plan, and we now spend weeks at a time living and working in a warmer climate during the winter months.

CULTIVATE YOUR CONTRIBUTIONS

Cultivate Your Contributions means focusing on the present: how can you build a strong team *now* to craft a solid financial future? This strategy encourages you to cultivate the best work by building your community. We all have unique worldviews, and what motivates us is inherently dynamic. Therefore, your planning process has to be equally dynamic to meet you there.

At Cedar Brook, we have created a community of advisors who bring fresh ideas and innovative strategies to the table every day. It was essential for us to foster a learning laboratory in which ideas could incubate and grow. We believe that the cross-pollination of intellectual capital becomes a multiplier for the most sound and creative solutions. I have my own perspective, knowledge, and life experience. Similarly, my partners at the firm each have distinctive experiences, outlooks, and knowledge, as do our outside partners who help our clients with estate planning, tax, and healthcare strategies. Our unique fingerprints all come with unique solutions for our existing clients, which is why we like to work as a team.

The same is true for our clients. We don't want to create their financial strategy in a vacuum. We want to partner with them on this journey. This leads to ideas that are regularly co-created. We believe the litmus test of a great planning process is what the advisor will do with the answers you've come up with in Mine Your Bliss. Planning is so multifaceted that, typically, there isn't one correct answer. If only one or a few advisors contribute to a financial plan, there's a finite amount of intellectual capital feeding that plan. So instead, we take all the groundwork you laid when Mining Your Bliss and use that information to Cultivate Your Contributions within a smart, supportive community. *That's* how we live in Shared Purpose with our clients and ourselves.

We conduct biweekly strategy sessions, often with over a dozen advisors in the room. The focus and creativity in these sessions are electric. We feed off each other, brainstorming refreshingly poignant ideas.

You can do the same. First, cultivate your contributions by working with an advisor and financial team that includes *you* in the planning process. Next, surround yourself with collaborators doing dynamic work in the field. Then, once you know you have a good team in place, invite and celebrate everyone's contributions.

THE LEADERSHIP LEVER

The third part, The Leadership Lever, is about your financial future. We know that a great plan is the beginning of the journey but not the destination. Many financial advisors promise an annual review, where you get a big binder with all your numbers. You review those numbers, life goes back to normal, and your aspirations get tucked away until next year.

We believe that for any endeavor to be successful, it must have consistent and active leadership at its core. The Leadership Lever speaks to our belief that planning is a lifelong journey— one that's rewarding and invigorating, not cumbersome or stressful. You and your advisor both need to play a leadership role in converting your dreams into your achievements.

Keep asking yourself: what's changed, what's new, and what's next? Sometimes your goals or vision change, so be sure to pause now and then to Mine Your Bliss. On the technical side of planning, changes occur in the tax, legal, financial, and economic realms. Make sure your advisor stays on top of those changes and knows how they are lining you up with your current goals.

Because we are committed to living in Shared Purpose with our clients, we know that's not enough. We push our clients throughout the year to figure out what they want for their future and how to make it a reality. Let's think back to Harold and Lydia from Chapter 1. One of their goals was to be able to spend a month at a time on the East Coast visiting their family. Our job was to use The Leadership Lever to make that happen.

PREPARE FOR AND CELEBRATE YOUR STORY

Our team constantly asks ourselves, "How do we add the most value for this client? How do we avoid going through the motions and appreciate each client's individual story?" I've included two worksheets that help us prepare for and celebrate with our clients at Cedar Brook.

Use this diagram to work on a project, or prepare for an internal or external meeting.
The Humanity Factor Unique Story serves as your thinking tool for preparation.

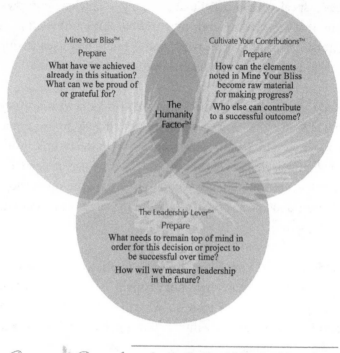

Mine Your Bliss™

Prepare

What have we achieved
already in this situation?
What can we be proud of
or grateful for?

Cultivate Your Contributions™

Prepare

How can the elements
noted in Mine Your Bliss
become raw material
for making progress?

Who else can contribute
to a successful outcome?

The
Humanity
Factor™

The Leadership Lever™

Prepare

What needs to remain top of mind in
order for this decision or project to
be successful over time?

How will we measure leadership
in the future?

At Cedar Brook, we use The Humanity Factor Prepare Diagram when meeting a client for the first time, before strategy sessions, and during annual reviews. This helps our team keep each individual's unique story at the forefront of our planning.

First, we Mine Our Bliss: What have we already achieved for this client? What can we be proud of or grateful for in that scenario? Then, we Cultivate Our Contributions: Is there anybody we can bring in that will add value to the client? Is it another partner or

The Humanity Factor™ | Celebrate

Use this diagram to work on a project, or prepare for an internal or external meeting.
The Humanity Factor Unique Story serves as your thinking tool for preparation.

Mine Your Bliss™

Celebrate

How did you take stock
of today: was it for yourself
or by helping a team member
or client do so for themselves?

What were your shared
experiences as a result?

The
Humanity
Factor™

Cultivate Your Contributions™

Celebrate

How were you able to
integrate the contributions
of individuals and teams
into the decision-making
cycle or solution
development?

What are you most proud
of regarding the outcome?

The Leadership Lever™

Celebrate

How do you plan to bring leadership
to the table over time in order to
influence a more powerful result
than might be present without
leadership as a committment?

Cedar Brook
GROUP
CULTIVATE TODAY.℠

Securities offered through Cadaret, Grant & Co., Inc., an SEC
Registered Investment Advisor and member FINRA/SIPC.
Advisory services offered through Cadaret, Grant & Co., Inc. and
Cedar Brook Group, an SEC Registered Investment Advisor.
Cadaret, Grant & Co. and Cedar Brook Group are separate entities.

resource within or outside of Cedar Brook that would benefit
their plan? Finally, we pull The Leadership Lever: What needs
to remain top of mind as we continue to help this client over
the next year? How can that be the raw material for what we
do next on their behalf?

You can use this to prepare for your own planning meetings and
reviews. But make sure to celebrate your wins along the way
with The Humanity Factor Celebrate Diagram. Don't let time

go by without recognizing the good you've done between those meetings. Celebrating gives you the clarity and confidence to keep pursuing your most ambitious goals.

COMBINING THE ELEMENTS OF YOUR UNIQUE STORY

Combining the three elements—Mine Your Bliss, Cultivate Your Contributions, and The Leadership Lever—is like planting seeds. At Cedar Brook, we love to watch those seeds potentially grow into deep, stable roots that may eventually bear fruit.

Let's consider two of my clients. Nick and Stephanie are a brilliant power couple in their mid-50s. Unfortunately, Nick was caught up in conventional wisdom, which meant he was hard on himself regarding the family's finances. Nick and Stephanie had a financial advisor they were working with who they weren't happy with, so they decided to check out Cedar Brook.

Nick and Stephanie were heads of departments at their respective Fortune 500 companies, and their workplaces were constantly changing, whether it be new bosses or new directives. Simultaneously, the bar kept getting raised higher and higher in their roles, and more and more was being asked of them. They were both being rewarded for it financially, but they were wearing golden handcuffs, and sometimes the stress of it all didn't seem worth it.

Ultimately, they were burnt out, and they both wanted financial independence to be possible sooner than later. When Nick and Stephanie came to us, they felt like they needed X number of dollars to get out of the rat race and became obsessed with getting on the other side to the point that it was impacting their health. They told us how the stress was affecting them and kept asking, "Why work this hard to retire when we're going to be too sick to enjoy it?" The couple felt like they needed to be doing something different with their savings so they could retire sooner, but they weren't necessarily sure where to start.

Instead of focusing on the dollar amount, we Mined Their Bliss by aligning their assets and resources to what they wanted to accomplish. We learned that the couple had two daughters and had already paid for their college education, which meant their children had graduated from university debt-free and landed good jobs. They were successfully launched! In Mining Their Bliss, we discovered Nick and Stephanie were in a great financial position and had a lot to be proud of.

But still, we had to ask the hard questions to the core of "why" they were working so hard. Through that exercise, they could see that the math looked good, and in that case, what was all of the stress really for? We got their nose out of the spreadsheet by getting to the heart of the matter. Suddenly, Nick and Stephanie felt gratitude for where they were and how they got there.

After we reflected on the "why," we moved into Cultivate Your Contributions. They realized they wanted to spend more time with their daughters and future grandchildren. And they wanted to pick up hobbies and passions they'd neglected while building their careers. They also loved to travel. They realized those simple goals were worth more than a couple of extra zeros on the balance sheet. We helped them work less and enjoy life more without sacrificing their retirement goals.

What we ended up creating for them was a bucket strategy

where—because they are young—longevity and sequence of return risk were a big issue. We did this by setting the first several years aside in cash for money they know they will spend, and another bucket of money was placed in fixed income to be used as the next pool of spending money. Then, the remainder was invested in a long-term growth strategy that could be left alone to grow over time.

By the time we moved into The Leadership Lever element, Nick and Stephanie found there was light at the end of the tunnel, and they knew it was within reach. Once a "work optional" life was on the horizon, their mindset changed. Now work was what they *chose* to do versus what they were *forced* to do.

When Nick and Stephanie walked through our door, they carried the world's weight on their shoulders. But by honoring their Unique Story, that weight holding them down disappeared.

Mining Their Bliss grounded them in being grateful for where they were, and being able to look to the future from a place of gratitude calmed them. They painted a picture of the future that aligned with their values and ambitions.

Cultivating Their Contributions was a bright spot for the couple since Nick is insightful about investing practices. He actively cultivated his contributions, which included bringing strategies and ideas to Cedar Brook.

The Leadership Lever element is ongoing. For example, we recently had a conversation where Nick and Stephanie asked if we could accelerate their retirement because of changes at both of their workplaces. Now, they're confident enough to retire earlier than expected, but when they walked into our office a few years ago, they thought retirement was a far-off dream.

Believe it or not, reducing the stress around money and improving your emotional well-being with a positive mindset helps you make better financial decisions. In the example of my wife's diagnoses, we will always be dealing with challenges beyond our control. But while you can't alter an unexpected challenge, you can alter how you think about it and manage the stress around it, financially and otherwise.

Consider Harold and Lydia again. Lydia still tells me that The Humanity Factor relieved her anxiety and gave her confidence. When Lydia was a new client, she confided she'd been losing sleep because of the state of her finances. We took her through this same process, and now she sleeps soundly at night.

When you're applying our approach, I hope you can see yourself in these examples. My goal is to help you identify things that have frustrated you and visualize a smoother path grounded in your intentions and values.

GOOD PLANNING EMBRACES CHANGE

Plans need to evolve because life changes. You never know when your job, your health, or the financial markets will be disrupted. So the goals you may have right now will always be dynamic, considering the changing factors that impact us all.

But it's not just about accounting for hard times and undesirable changes. It's also about welcoming new blessings and unexpected joys, like twin grandchildren or the chance to move cross-country to live near your son. As you achieve some of your goals, others will shift. It's essential to track these changes and ensure your plan does too. A healthy, evolving financial plan will allow you to dream bigger and bigger along the way.

WHO WILL YOU BE IN RETIREMENT?

As you're going through this process, I want you to ask yourself, "In an ideal world, how would I like to spend my time?" Think about that in the present and the future. Use this to help you think through who you are on the other side of retirement, even if retirement is down the road.

When it comes to how they'd like to spend their time in retirement, you'd be shocked at how many people have never considered it. People too focused on money and savings often get into retirement and lose their sense of identity, partly because they haven't thought about what they'll do when they retire. When your career or savings account becomes your identity, it becomes difficult to enjoy life when that identity changes.

Rather than focus on *how* they want to spend their time post-retirement, people tend to only fixate on their retirement date. They daydream about it and repeatedly talk to their spouse or advisor about that date. But so many people don't think about what retirement looks like six months after that date comes and goes.

The less thought that's given, the more risk the person will be unhappy or unsettled when they get to that six-month mark. It's crucial to think through what life will look like after you stop working: who are you then?

USING YOUR UNIQUE STORY TO FIND FULFILLMENT

Using your Unique Story to take the focus off the numbers, you can imagine the life you want to lead, and we can create a financial plan that guides you toward that goal. Going through this process pushes you to measure the right way by taking stock of your past successes and strengths so we can leverage those gains into the building blocks of a solid future, and then keep it going and evolving.

When people align their resources with their values, there is immense fulfillment. People stop sweating the small stuff. They stop ruminating on things they don't have any control over because they're focusing on the things they do have control over—which is how they spend their time and what they do with their life.

It's possible that when you picked up this book, you felt like you were on a path where you would have to work forever and that every day would be a grind. I hope you're starting to see now that it doesn't need to be that way. Financial independence is an option for you, and you can have it alongside clarity and comfort.

Right now, you may be thinking, "All of this sounds great, but what if unknowns begin to spoil the good financial plan I'm developing?"

Next, we'll get into just that—because sometimes, planning for the future is also about preparing for those unknowns.

CHAPTER 3

Transforming Dangers

So many people have already won the money game; they're on their way. You're likely winning too. But, as you develop your Unique Story and find answers to what drives you, you may also discover some fears regarding your savings. By taking a closer look at the unknowns, you can help ensure you don't lose a game you've already won.

When I say *fears*, I'm not talking about things like, "I'm scared I'm not smart enough to come up with the right financial plan" or "I'm fearful I don't have the willpower to save." If you doubt yourself with statements like that, I encourage you to dismiss them immediately. Anyone can come up with—and execute— an excellent plan as long as they get out of their own way.

The fears I'm referring to are *not* those related to money-saving or mindset but instead are the unknown obstacles. They're the things that can potentially spoil an otherwise concrete retire-ment plan. These fears are the ones that jolt you out of bed at 2 a.m.: "What if I lose my job?", "What if markets go down?", or "What happens if my spouse dies and I can't afford the bills?"

People tend to avoid planning for the things that scare them because it means discussing uncomfortable subjects. But as you might guess, The Humanity Factor encourages you to do just that. In fact, as a company, we like to say, "the obstacle is the way."[4] We find that obstacles can be useful if you simply address them in advance.

Let me explain. If you created a goal for yourself to retire at a specific time, you might ask, "What am I certain about, and what am I uncertain about?"[5] Your uncertainties *are* the obstacles. You may be worried about a recession, market performance, or how your portfolio will perform after you retire. But you're also concerned about things more significant and personal: losing your job, experiencing a loss in your family, a natural disaster, a costly health event, another pandemic, or a divorce. These are just a few examples of the things that keep people up at night.

Addressing those uncertainties can be intimidating, but tackling the obstacles head-on is the way to ensure they don't spoil a good plan. A holistic financial plan accounts for unexpected life events. We can deal with the numbers now, so you have the space you need to live fully and presently when difficulties arise down the road.

---

4   Ryan Holiday, *The Obstacle Is the Way: The Timeless Art of Turning Trials into Triumph* (New York: Penguin/Portfolio, 2014).

5   To learn more about the "Certainty/Uncertainty filter," a Dan Sullivan strategic coach tool, visit www.strategiccoach.com.

You cannot prepare for how the loss of a loved one will impact you or your family emotionally. But you can mitigate the financial impact. The next hard time shouldn't undo your entire life.

I met Miriam years ago. She came to Cedar Brook when her husband died unexpectedly. Before he passed away, Miriam was a stay-at-home mom, and her husband, Patrick, owned a business. They were a young couple with three small children, so they didn't have a lifetime of savings. Still, Patrick worked hard to grow his business, and the couple invested in life insurance. They had a plan for the kind of life they wanted to live, but when Patrick passed away in his forties, that life was gone. His death gutted Miriam and their children.

A financial plan couldn't take away their suffering, but Miriam's family had something to be thankful for: the thought Miriam and Patrick put into their future. In the months after Patrick's passing, Miriam had the space to grieve and support her children. It would have been a gut-wrenching time for her to wonder, "Do I have to sell the house? How quickly do I have to find work?" During those critical first months, her kids needed her.

Miriam and Patrick's financial plan gave her the time and space to be with her children in the aftermath of a crisis. During a challenging moment, your plan will allow you to focus on the essential things and potentially avoid basic security fears like, "Will I be able to put food on the table or keep a roof over my family's head?"

This chapter aims to help you prepare for whatever obstacles you're fearful of so that you can put them out of your mind and *live.* I ask you to be honest with yourself so that we can get to what scares you the most—and then plan for it.

POOR MARKET PERFORMANCE CAN SPOIL A GOOD PLAN

A common topic people fear when they step into our office is the market's instability—it's a constant unknown. Our risk-averse clients live in fear of how market changes might negatively impact them and their families.

For instance, my clients on the verge of retirement worry about how the market will perform when they stop collecting a paycheck and start living off their savings. If the market tanks, does that mean they won't be able to help with their grandchildren's education as they hoped?

Consider the Sequence of Return Risk. When you're in the Accumulation Phase, you are accumulating your wealth by collecting a paycheck and making retirement plan and other contributions. During this phase, studies have shown it doesn't matter what order the returns on your investments are because you aren't withdrawing those funds.[6] But when you retire, you enter the Distribution Phase, and at that point, when and how you take out money significantly impacts your financial future.

Think of it like this: in the Distribution Phase, let's say that your portfolio is down 22 percent for the year. So, if you're taking 5 percent of your saved money out to live on in retirement, you're now in the red 27 percent. This deficit makes it very difficult to

---

6   "Understanding How Returns and Withdrawals May Impact a Portfolio," John Hancock Life Insurance Company, 2008, https://www.devolfinancial.com/files/48836/Sequence%20of%20Returns-1.pdf.

get back to where you started and impacts your ability to stay at a steady pace of withdrawing from your retirement accounts for the remainder of your retirement. As you can imagine, this unknown causes anxiety.

For clients fearful of market changes, we help them potentially avoid this by creating a Segmentation Strategy, which, as the name suggests, is composed of three distinct segments. In the first segment, we estimate what money they'll need in order to get through the first couple of years of spending in retirement. We set those funds aside in cash, so it doesn't matter what the market is doing during those years for these dollars—that money is safe from market risk. That way, if the client picks the wrong year to retire in terms of market performance, it won't matter. The second segment is a pool of savings that's more conservative. It serves as the next segment of money the family will use to pay for living expenses. This segment is designed to address your intermediate time horizon needs/goals. Finally, the third segment is made up of long-term investments that *are* affected by the market. However, since these funds are designed for longevity, the client doesn't have to worry if the market goes through a hard time because they don't need to withdraw that money at a particular time. Instead, they can pull from the prior two segments and save their long-term investments for an unspecified future date.

Of course, these are generalizations because financial plans are specific to each family and their needs. However, this is just one of many examples that illustrate how we help clients who are fearful of market-related obstacles.

Planning for market instability helps people stop fixating on an investment app so they can go out and live their life. You don't want to spend your retirement agonizing over the day-to-day swings in the market—an external factor you simply have no control over. The Humanity Factor allows you to enjoy your life, retirement, family, goals, and hobbies, knowing that you've planned for obstacles.

DON'T LOSE A GAME YOU'VE ALREADY WON

Some people are on the other end of the spectrum—they don't fear the market at all. Instead, they're laser-focused on aggressively increasing the number in their account. It's important to them to do better than the market or some other index they're chasing—and they want to go for it despite the potential risk of losing half of their money in a volatile market.

We challenge these numbers-driven clients to consider their Unique Story. If they are aggressively investing in the market but also trying to save for their grandchildren's education, does it really make sense to risk it all? We like to say, "You can't hug a spreadsheet." Don't make everything about the returns.

We also tell clients: Don't lose a game you've already won. If you're already ahead, why risk it? If your family has the money it needs to live comfortably for the rest of your life, you wouldn't want to invest it in a way that could change the math, right?

Now, let's get back to *you*. Are you currently winning? The answer is probably "yes," and a good financial strategy can show you how to keep it that way. Don't risk all that you've built by ignoring unforeseen obstacles or chasing risky returns.

CONTROL THE CONTROLLABLE

If you're someone who has yet to retire, I want you to try something: Mentally fast-forward three years from now.[7] Come up with a list of things that need to happen between now and then for you to feel comfortable and confident with where you are in your life. This list should include the things you want to be true for your bigger future. Define those things clearly, and then take action toward them.

So, if you want to save at a consistent rate, automate your savings to make that happen; you can take control of that today. If you want to eliminate some pesky debt, create and follow a debt repayment plan, like the snowball or avalanche methods. That's another thing you can control right now.

Then, I want you to look at what you've written down and see if there are any obstacles to achieving these goals. Come up with solutions for those obstacles now, in advance of them ever happening.

By controlling the controllable, you're solving problems logically and rationally now instead of during a high-stress, emotionally-charged moment in your life.

PREPARING FOR THE WORST

My mother-in-law grew up in a household that was comfortable financially, as her dad owned a successful business. But when he passed away unexpectedly, everything changed. Because they

---

7   Dan Sullivan, *The Dan Sullivan Question: Ask it and Transform Anyone's Future* (Toronto: The Strategic Coach, Inc., 2009).

hadn't planned for a worst-case scenario, his death left their family in financial turmoil.

Because of this, my mother-in-law became fearful this would happen when she had a family of her own. So she was focused on planning ahead. She was determined never to go through what her family had gone through, so when she married her husband, Mike (my wife's father), she prioritized financial security, which included taking out life insurance policies in case of tragedy.

Then, sadly, that day came. At only forty years old, my wife's father, Mike, died of a massive heart attack. While the death was traumatizing for the family, my mother-in-law took comfort in knowing they wouldn't have to deal with financial collapse on top of the shock and emotional stress. This is one of the personal stories that I take to heart when creating a plan for myself or others. It serves as a guiding principle every day.

One of my clients, James, is someone whose preparedness for financial obstacles has given him solace in the face of great adversity. James met a girl named Sophie in grade school. They became high school sweethearts and married after college. After that, James enlisted in the army, and while he was serving, they had three sons. Eventually, James left the military and landed a job at a company where he worked his way up the ladder to a director of sales position.

Throughout their marriage, they made a middle-class living. Despite their modest income, James and Sophie put $50 a month into a mutual fund account for each of their boys, trying to nickel and dime their way to some savings. James and Sophie were responsible savers and knew the importance of long-term investments. Still, there wasn't a ton of disposable income, but they tried to be good stewards of their resources and always prepared for the "what-if."

James and Sophie learned that private equity investors were interested in buying the company where James worked, so the couple decided to take a big risk. They took out a home equity loan to invest in his company, hoping to get a return if the company sold.

One Friday night, not long after that, the couple was heading to their son's football game when James noticed that Sophie was jaundiced. Alarmed, they went to the hospital and later discovered that Sophie had pancreatic cancer. Her prognosis was grim. James did as much research as possible to improve her situation, and Sophie underwent aggressive treatments, but in the end, she succumbed to her illness. James and his sons were devastated.

What happened next was bittersweet. Just two weeks after Sophie's death, James's company sold. He made millions of dollars from the investment he and Sophie made together. For most people, this would be a celebratory moment, but James felt a sense of loss and guilt that his high school sweetheart and life partner wasn't there to see their hard work and dedication come to fruition.

We met with James not long after that challenging period in his life. He eventually joined our firm to help our clients with closely held businesses. While working with us, James shared his personal story with my colleagues and me. We could tell that he was heartbroken that Sophie never had the chance to share in their good fortune, but we also knew that couldn't possibly be true—James could walk through The Humanity Factor as a way to include Sophie's legacy in his financial plan.

Now James works with us not only as a consultant but also as a client. As his advisor and colleague, I recognize how important it is for their family's financial plan to honor Sophie's legacy. During our strategy meetings, James asks, "What would Sophie want me to do?" Over the years, we answered this question by funding their sons' educations, helping them buy their first homes, and starting college education accounts for their grandchildren.

James also donated to the local elementary school he and Sophie attended so the school could build a beautiful new playground for future generations of children. Sophie always loved the church bells at their parish, and they broke a few years after her passing. Without hesitation, James donated a generous sum to have them repaired. Every time he hears the sound of those bells, they remind James of Sophie. For James, this was money well spent.

We continue to apply The Humanity Factor to every aspect of James's financial plan, staying centered on his unique and poignant "why," which is to honor his late wife and their family legacy. This allows James to celebrate all he and Sophie accomplished during their marriage and to include her legacy as a central part of his shared purpose with us. When we met James he was still grieving, but this process helped set his sights on his bigger future, one where his family remains financially secure. That security allows James and his sons to grieve without the fear they'll lose their home or go into debt.

Planning for obstacles and being a good steward of their resources did not change the outcome of James's and Sophie's life, but it did allow James to create something good out of difficult circumstances. James's story teaches us that being prepared for obstacles cannot eliminate all of your risks or fears. But it also proves that preparation allows you to live your values and purpose should those obstacles arise. James and Sophie talked about these things while she was alive, so James knew what to do. That is the power of conversation and relationship.

GETTING VULNERABLE ABOUT YOUR FINANCIAL FEARS

Planning provides immense confidence for people. Consider my client, Meghan. She's a doctor with two sons, one of whom has schizophrenia. Because of the severity of his condition, he has to live in a mental health home where he can receive 24/7 access to healthcare professionals. The family also receives aid from the state because of his diagnosis and inability to work or care for himself. Meghan pays the remainder of the cost out of her current savings.

When Meghan came to us, she was scared of the unknowns her son might face when she was gone. So, we got real with her. We asked her what worried her the most. As with all of our clients, we told Meghan that the more honest she was upfront, the more we'd be able to help.

Meghan's greatest fear was what would happen when she passed away, and her son had no provider. She was terrified of her son being alone without a safety net. She wanted to ensure a secure and stable financial transition for her son should anything happen to her. So, we took her list and brought clarity and awareness to every single one of her concerns. Together, we analyzed what could go wrong and discussed solutions for each potential obstacle.

Knowing Meghan's Unique Story and her fears, we worked with our outside attorney partners, who established a special needs trust. The trust ensures that Meghan's son continues to receive the same level of care once she's gone and that his state benefits will not be interrupted. The trust also allows Cedar Brook to help guide her son's financial plan in the future, too. Meghan wants to know that powerful allies are in her son's corner after she's gone, and we take that responsibility seriously.

The hardest part for Meghan was being vulnerable enough to discuss her fears with us. But in doing just that, she received confidence knowing she is doing everything she can. She's controlling the controllable. Now, she's in the driver's seat instead of feeling like the *unknowns* are guiding her life.

It can be difficult to get vulnerable with a financial advisor, particularly regarding their fears. People don't necessarily associate us with emotions—after all, financial plans are supposed to be unsentimental. But as you know by now, that's not how The Humanity Factor works. It goes beyond the typical financial planning approach to create professional intimacy.

As you were open to sharing your Unique Story, you must also be open to sharing your fears with your advisor. And if your advisor hasn't taken your obstacles seriously, get a new one who will actively listen to and address your concerns.

OVERCOMING YOUR POTENTIAL OBSTACLES

Now that you're aware of some common financial fears and how people plan for them, you can begin to do the same for your own potential obstacles.

Ask yourself:

- What keeps me up at night? A market downturn, the loss of a loved one, a health scare, inflation, or losing my job?
- Do some fears feel more pressing, urgent, or likely than others?
- Do I have any unique circumstances, like Meghan?

Once you've identified your obstacles, start thinking about the steps needed to mitigate them.

For each concern or obstacle, outline:

- What questions do I need to ask to address this fear?
- What can I start doing today to address this potential obstacle? (How can I control the controllable?)
- Do any of my potential obstacles require insight from a professional?

Some people will feel uncomfortable thinking about the possibility of adverse events. Remember, you can plan for worst-case scenarios by identifying dangers. Wouldn't you rather be prepared, just in case?

Addressing your fears is not just good; it's critical. It means you can commit to doing things differently *today* to best prepare for anything that comes your way *tomorrow*. Preparation allows you to experience life without added stress.

And I've got some good news, too: once you've eaten your vegetables, you get to have dessert. After you've addressed your fears in *this* chapter, you get to dream about what's possible once you create a plan to move on from those fears in the next chapter. You've earned the right to stop thinking about what you might lose and start getting excited about what you can gain!

In the next chapter, you get to ask yourself, "Now that I've made a plan for my obstacles, what can I focus on that enlivens me?" Is it more time with your family or purchasing a vacation home? Maybe it's travel, charitable giving, or the opportunity to work on creative projects. What about a more flexible work schedule? As you can see, there is much to gain once you've put the right plan in place.

CHAPTER 4

Maximizing Opportunities

As far back as I can remember, I was known to bug my parents for little jobs I could do around the house to make money. I knew even back then that I needed money if I wanted to be able to buy the things I wanted: baseball cards, baseball hats, and helmet sundaes from Baskin Robbins. (Notice a theme?) When I was fourteen years old, I got my first real job as a busboy at a local restaurant so that I had the resources to keep buying what I wanted and to afford to be able to do my favorite activities, too. I loved walking out of there every night with cash in hand. I still remember the satisfaction I felt after buying my first baseball hat. It was the first thing I'd ever bought on my own. I think of that all these years later when I put one on.

I guess I've always been a dollars and cents guy, but if you weren't the type to practice those habits of earning money to yield a reward when you were a kid, that definitely doesn't mean you can't implement those habits now as an adult. Anyone can create a plan for themselves that allows them to be smart about how they accumulate, save, and spend money on necessities so that there is extra money left over to be spent on meaningful things they enjoy.

IT'S TIME TO DREAM BIG

In the last chapter, we talked in detail about financial fears—those unknowns that may pop up and spoil your financial plan. It's essential to have transformed your dangers in the last chapter so that you feel comfortable and confident with where you are in life. Now that we've addressed your dangers, we can think about what's possible after all that is said and done; the things you can *gain*. Your gains are the positive things—the rewards—that you'll be able to take away from your plan. They're the dividends that allow you to spend time on hobbies you love or allow you to take that vacation you've always wanted to go on, or anything else you've dreamt of. We can help make those dreams become a reality.

Once you know that you're on track financially and that mom and dad are going to be okay, then we get to ask a question you might not be expecting: what would make life even better?

Generally, when people come to us, they just want to ensure they can do two things: pay their expenses and retire. When we're able to show them they can do more than just *exist*, that's when the conversation turns. Clients will look to their partner and say, "You know, we've always talked about having a summer home."

Sometimes it's about grandkids: living closer, spending more time together, helping with their education, or a big family trip to Disney or their country of origin. Sometimes it's just practical: "Hey, why don't we bake in an extra thousand dollars a month in pocket money?"

A good way to start uncovering the things you're yearning to have and do is to ask yourself:

- What would I be spending on and/or doing if money and time were not an object?
- What would I do if I weren't nagged by the daily routine of just trying to keep up?

We like to tell our clients to think back to the eight-year-old version of themselves and ask: *What would he/she be doing right now? What would that kid be spending their earnings on?*

There are likely at least a few things you wanted to spend time doing as an eight-year-old that are still on your wishlist. When I was eight, all I wanted to do was get on my bike, meet my buddies, and, of course, play baseball. Translated into my adult life, you can still find me spending my extra time and money watching the Cleveland Guardians (formerly Indians, still getting used to it) play at Progressive Field or at a local park watching my nieces and nephew play like I did when Reese was playing.

Now, consider how your inner eight-year-old translates to your life now. Do you want more time off in the summers to go on beach trips? Do you want to be working at all? Do you want to do more philanthropy or have more time to engage with your community? Is it important to retire early so you can spend more time with your loved ones?

Sometimes the answers yield something quite grand, and sometimes it's something really small and simple, but regardless, these rewards you're seeking should be unique to you. Often, the answers will point people to the fact that they want that extra free time to spend time with those they love. That love motivates them and serves to improve the quality of those relationships. That's something that applies to most people in the world, no matter who you are.

YOUR DREAMS ARE A GATEWAY TO CLARITY, CONFIDENCE–AND SUCCESS

Answering these questions helps bring extra clarity to your dreams, ambitions, and values so that you can create a plan that moves you closer to your *gains* instead of just living in the status quo. So many people keep their heads down, make their 401(k) contributions, and then find themselves in a position where they're *more* successful than they thought they would be. You would think they'd be happy to hear that, but these folks have spent so much time and energy focused on accumulating their wealth that it can be hard for them to enjoy it.

In a later chapter, we're going to focus on putting together a Sample Financial Plan for you, and that plan will be really important. Because we have to show our work and say, "I'm not making this up—the numbers prove you're on track for your goals. Now that we know you're on track, how can we take you further?"

For me, those moments are the best. I see visible relief in clients: their shoulders relax and their smiles light up the room. You can feel their sense of accomplishment about the past and genuine excitement about the future.

Saving and planning are about more than just accumulating. You'll make better financial decisions if you connect to the fruits of your labor. That's why it pays to get to know yourself and your ambitions—and make sure your advisor knows them, too, because different life goals impact your strategy.

At Cedar Brook, we learn what makes our clients' hearts go pitter-patter before we model out their unique plans. Maybe it's purchasing another property, traveling, or setting money aside for their grandchildren's education. When we get to this point, we run the hard numbers.

Sometimes we get to say, "You can take that trip right now." Other times, our team gathers with a pot of coffee to create a strategy. During these brainstorming sessions, we focus on connecting our client's resources with their possibilities. That's why we emphasize that "your future is bigger than your past." This is about rooting your plan in bedrock fundamentals like longevity, contentment, and purpose so you can enjoy a fuller tomorrow.

If you're not looking at your plan from the lens of your values and goals, that's corrosive conventional wisdom. It doesn't matter if Financial Company A or your neighbors are doing their plan differently. Who cares? What matters is that you are the central figure in your planning and that the only thing you are just accountable for is yourself and your family.

You don't have to think about your values and ambitions while making a financial plan, but why *wouldn't* you? We don't want you to reflect back on your life and say, "You know, I wish we would have taken that trip."

I don't want you to live with any regret. Instead, I want you to maximize your hard work, family history, and relationships and make the most of what you have so you can dream even bigger. Sometimes in our conversations with clients, they're skeptical of this. They think it can't be real that they'd be able to pay their expenses, plan for the future, *and still* have money left over for the fun stuff. Most of the time, though, clients love these conversations. It opens their eyes to opportunities they hadn't thought about in years.

We get why our more conservative clients get nervous about dreaming big in terms of rewards. They may have trained their minds at various points in their lives to not get overly excited at the potential of good things coming to fruition for them because they ask themselves, "What happens if those things didn't work out?" We say, why not let the positive thoughts in? Why not allow *them* to flood your brain? There's no harm in planning for the potential gains and telling yourself that you can have them.

YOUR PLAN CAN MOVE YOU TOWARD YOUR PURPOSE
EVA'S STORY

This is your life, it shouldn't just be about money. It should be about the things you love. My client, Eva, and her husband, Ted, both work full-time. They have three children, two of whom are successfully launched, and the third is entering college. Eva and Ted are both successful; she is a sought-after consultant. Eva has many demands on her time. She's a wife, mother, and business professional, but she's always made it a point to volunteer with an organization she cares deeply about, one that brings her a lot of joy, Big Hearted Blooms.

Big Hearted Blooms is a nonprofit that repurposes flowers that are used in churches for various events, like weddings, funerals, or other celebrations in the church throughout the year. They use the flowers that would have otherwise been disposed of, repurposing them by bringing them to people in hospitals and nursing homes to brighten their day. The flowers go to patients going through particularly difficult times health-wise, those who aren't being visited by family or friends, or patients who feel isolated, sick, or scared. Eva has always loved gardening, so she loves the aspect of caring for the flowers, and of course, she also loves bringing other people joy in the process. It's a win-win and has made her fall in love with this organization.

We learned this information about Eva when we'd gone through The Humanity Factor™ and got to the softer questions, like "What does retirement look like for you?" She talked at length about wanting to spend more of her time with the organization in retirement since she loves every minute of it. We then made sure we focused her and Ted's plan around that and put numbers behind it.

Eva knows how precious time is. She is a breast cancer survivor, so she lives with a life-changing diagnosis in the back of her mind. She goes for her regular scans and check-ups to stay on top of things in recovery, but she wants to get to the good stuff faster. She's not someone who wants to wait to do the things she truly enjoys. We've seen this many times with clients. When faced with their worst fears, people start caring far less about whether Mutual Fund A will perform better than Mutual Fund B. They just want to live their life—and maximize their opportunities.

So, that became important to Eva's plan. We helped her come up with ways she could get there faster since volunteer work was such a big passion of hers. We were able to align her resources with that priority.

By letting Cedar Brook in on how important Big Hearted Blooms is to her, we could easily identify Eva's purpose. When it came to deciding how much to save or spend or how aggressive or conservative she should be with her money, philanthropy was her driving force. Changing your perspective to one of working toward a special reward will greatly impact your financial decisions and outlook. Suddenly, the numbers become less meaningful.

It's not to say the numbers aren't important. Everyone should still be good stewards of their resources if they want to reap their own benefits, but as with everything we've discussed with The Humanity Factor, purpose—and the things you *want* to work toward—is at the center of all of this.

SOREN AND PATRICIA'S STORY

Another couple, Soren and Patricia, are clients of ours who have lived in Cleveland forever. Their daughter attended Miami University, where she met her future husband (another successful Miami Merger!), and the two of them now have children of their own. They've made a life for themselves in Cincinnati, five hours from Cleveland. Like many grandparents, Soren and Patricia want to be able to spend time with their grandchildren and want to watch them grow up. They want to be there when the kids start playing T-ball and for lots of other events in their lives.

Soren and Patricia decided to dip their toes in the water and rent an apartment, under a one-year lease, near their daughter in Cincinnati. They take two weeks at a time to go and stay at the apartment, then they head home for two weeks and stay at their house, and repeat the cycle. Being able to spend time with their grandchildren like this, they knew they wanted—and *needed*—more of it. It broke their hearts every time their grandchildren would say, "Why do you have to leave? Can't you just *stay*, Nana and Papa?"

Not to mention, when they're in Cincinnati, it takes a lot of pressure off their daughter and son-in-law, both of whom travel for work. It's helpful to know that when things come up, the grandparents are right around the corner to help out with the kids.

Soren and Patricia came to us, laid this all out, and told us they're now interested in selling their house in Cleveland and buying a place to live in Cincinnati full-time. Their first question to us was, "Can we do it?" Then, they asked, "And if we *can* do it, what can we reasonably afford to buy?"

We were able to take this goal, match it to their numbers, and prove to them that they could absolutely make living near their grandchildren a reality. We showed them the concrete numbers to prove they could make this decision with confidence, knowing it will not negatively impact their futures. Now, they're excited about their decision to move, and we relieved a lot of that nervousness they had when they entered our office for that conversation.

Like Soren and Patricia, I recommend you dream big and allow those dreams to be realized. After all of the hard work you put in to prepare and save, don't you think you deserve to have and do the things you always wanted? Sometimes people are afraid to dream because they are afraid the answer will be "No." But why not take a chance and find out? Even if the answer *is* no, there could be an alternative solution, and you might be able to experience the thing you want, only in a different way. And it will be equally as meaningful.

What money really does—just like it did for me as a kid—is offer you a resource to get what you want and pursue your purpose. For Eva, money allows her to retire sooner so she can continue bringing that joy to her community in a hobby she loves. For Soren and Patricia, money is a tool that will allow them to spend more time with the people they love.

SO THEN, WHAT ARE *YOUR* DREAMS?

Stop and really think about your answers to these questions:

- What can I begin to do *now* to dream big?
- If I could have or do *anything,* what would it be?

Start to open up your imagination, and keep it going. As you look at your own numbers and create a plan to make your wishes come true, you'll find happiness and confidence. And then, after you achieve one of your *gains,* start to think about what you want your next reward to be. You'll also find added motivation to be good with your money because you'll be clear on *why* you're saving.

Think of this whole topic as you would a rewards system. It

works the same way it might with a child, for instance. If you incentivize your son or daughter to do something they don't necessarily want to do, it can suddenly feel exciting for them. So, if you tell them they can play outside with their friends after they clean their room, they're likely to clean that room pretty quickly, right? It's because they're eager and excited to get outside.

Maybe the process of working and saving doesn't necessarily *seem* fun to you, but isn't it exciting when you know there's a reward at the end—one that you, and only you, have clearly defined?

If you're still having trouble figuring out what the rewards would be for you, I again encourage you to ask yourself: What *would* your inner eight-year-old want to do?

Then, let's go from there!

CHAPTER 5

Reinforcing Strengths

At Cedar Brook, we like to say, "Planning for having enough money in retirement is just a high school math problem." Now that we've gotten through the personal aspects of The Humanity Factor™ and outlined your motivations, we can see how that math problem equates to you specifically.

That simple math, which we will get to in greater detail in the next chapter, tells us what's needed once the paychecks stop. After retirement, how much money will be required to cover your expenses and to achieve other objectives you set for yourself?

As we're calculating these numbers, what you'll find is that you will have certain strengths that benefit your situation and increase your confidence. If you're in a position to take stock of what you have and think about your future, then you already have good things happening, whether you clearly see them or not. Understanding and acknowledging current strengths will help you dream bigger and build a brighter future.

We'll use this chapter as a means of getting you to identify your strengths—your successes, attributes, and relationships—so that you can use them as a valuable resource and parlay your strengths into your success.

GIVE YOURSELF CREDIT

Sometimes our clients have difficulty seeing the strengths they bring to the table when it comes to planning. Even the most obvious things, like keeping expenses low, can be overlooked or underappreciated. But the truth is, really drawing on your strengths will lay the foundation for a healthy financial future.

Before we cover some common strengths, I want to quickly remind you how important it is to give yourself credit. Don't beat yourself up if you feel you have none of these strengths. A lot of people have a long runway, which means you have time to course-correct if needed. Be honest with yourself, as you've been throughout all of our previous lessons, and don't let a lack of confidence or modesty play against you, as it does for some people. Be excited to recognize your strengths, take stock of them, and use them to your advantage.

STRENGTHS THAT BENEFIT YOUR FINANCIAL FUTURE

Let's review some of the most common financial strengths and see if any resonate with you:

A positive, gracious attitude: Mental attitude is crucial in financial planning. Those who tend to stay positive and grateful for what they have saved and their accomplishments are eons ahead of the game. A positive mindset gets you to stop beating yourself up over past mistakes and to stop comparing yourself to the Joneses. It gets you to stop saying things like, "Fidelity did a study, and people aged 35 normally have X amount of dollars saved, but *I* don't." Who cares what other people are doing? Remember, this is all about *you* and your goals.

Good money habits: This goes without saying, but sometimes people need a reminder of how important good money habits are. If you are deliberate about how you spend your money and how much you save, you have a competitive advantage—there's no doubt about it. It will take you a shorter time to work toward retirement, and you'll have more in the bank when you do.

Low expenses: Building off good money habits and being a good steward of your family's money is also an incredible strength. Keeping your expenses low reduces the pile of money you need to have later in life. If you're someone who is able to keep your expenses down to $50,000 a year instead of $250,000 a year, for example, you are much more likely to outlive your savings. There's that simple high school math again!

Dual income: Naturally, a dual income is another huge strength in planning. This is especially true when a couple has collectively thought through how they want to spend life beyond work so their retirement plan is cohesive.

A pension: If you're lucky enough to be in a job with a pension, like a teacher or another government job, then you can make a similar wage to someone who works a traditional office job while having to put away far less for the same retirement. Your pot of money saved can be significantly smaller. Since many people do not have pensions, I always suggest clients pay close attention to a company's match or retirement contribution. If you work for a company with a generous one, that's a huge strength, too, as long as you're taking advantage of it (e.g., contributing as much as you can to get the full match). It will help you get where you want to be much faster.

Good education: A good education is a financial strength that makes you employable, marketable, and in demand. It also helps bring in extra money. Let's say you graduated college around the age of twenty-two and worked until the traditional retirement age of sixty-five—that's forty-three years of income. If a college-educated person earns a certain percentage more per year than someone who is not college-educated, that extra money adds up a lot over that forty-plus-year span of working.

Saving from a young age: If you're someone who started saving at an early age, you're also ahead of the game. Consider the difference between beginning to make Roth IRA contributions at the age of twenty-five versus the age of thirty-five. As the accompanying graphic suggests, the benefits from starting contributions ten years sooner gives you a significant leg up. In fact, someone who maxes out their IRA contributions from twenty-five to thirty-five and then stops will have a larger nest egg than the same person who makes the same contributions beginning at thirty-five until sixty-five, using the same rate of return assumption. That's stunning. Every bit counts over the years, so we encourage clients to have their children start getting serious about saving as early as they can once they're employed. Even small amounts over a long period of time can turn into large amounts of money down the road.

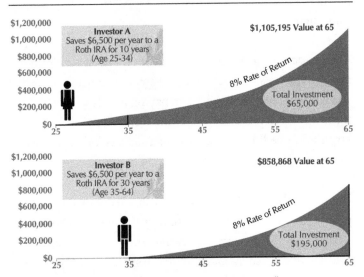

Growth rate chosen is for illustrative purposes only and does not reflect any past or future portfolio composition or performance of any specific investment.

Family history of resilience: When a family accomplishes a goal, they check it off their list and say, "Great! What's next?" But life is constantly throwing challenges our way. When a family experiences some kind of turmoil and gets through it by coming together, they build resilience. Shared experience brings them together, and that resilience prepares them for the next inevitable hard time. If your family is resilient, it'll help you bounce back, no matter what challenges arise financially.

Lack of debt: Simply put, without debt, you have extra monthly funds that you can save instead of allocating them to additional bills. There are obvious debts—like paying off any credit cards or personal loans—but as we get closer to retirement, we also talk to our clients about the added flexibility they'll have if they don't have a line item for a mortgage, too. Relieving those bigger payments and being debt-free offers much more flexibility in retirement.

A high-paying job: The more income you have, the more choices you'll have about your retirement as a whole and what you'll be able to afford. A higher-paying job allows you to save more while also preventing you from thinking twice about other essentials, like life or disability insurance or other important things people may skimp on.

The funny thing is, lots of people won't recognize their high-paying job as a strength because they'll complain about taxes, let's say. They'll also cite the lifestyle they got themselves into with a bigger paycheck and that they're spending to their level of income. They'll feel like they're stuck where they are and have to continue making that high income to keep their lifestyle. We, of course, encourage people in these situations to be conscious of their expenses. If they pair a low spend with a high income—it's a dream combination for retirement.

A solid career: When I say "solid career," I mean one with longevity and stability—it's having a career that is unlikely to be impacted, no matter what is happening in the economy. In advisors' eyes, a solid career is less prone to things like layoffs.

New capabilities and knowledge: If you have a specific skill set or knowledge, don't underestimate how that positively impacts your financial standing. The more value you bring to your job, the stronger your place there—and that applies across any industry. If you're able to solve problems others can't and you maximize opportunities, you'll be in demand, less likely to experience a layoff, and therefore less likely to be without a paycheck.

Your own successful business: Owning your own successful business is the holy grail. It's a strength like this that dictates how so much wealth has been built in our country. A successful business combines a potentially high income with an asset that can be sold, not to mention there are a lot of helpful tax and retirement planning strategies that can save business owners on expenses and increase how much they can save in retirement plans and outside investments. All of this provides a lot of flexibility with their planning.

Automating: If you're someone who automates their savings—you set it and forget it—you're doing something very powerful. Automation includes strategies like a monthly saving program, a monthly investing program, and/or paying your mortgage off biweekly instead of monthly (which can save a lot of interest).

A strong network of contacts: This is incredibly helpful in terms of navigating your finances. If you find yourself in trouble, one of the most powerful things we can do for each other is make connections. It's social capital, and it makes you more marketable, too, because it makes you a referable employee. Introducing someone who can help solve a problem or clean up a mess for someone else is one of the most powerful things we can do for one another.

Quality relationships: Beyond a large network of contacts, having quality relationships with a few of those people is also an incredible strength. It simplifies saving time and money at certain points in your life. For example, if you've developed a quality relationship with a lawyer, and unexpected legal trouble comes your way, you're able to pick up the phone and get assistance from someone you know and trust instead of having to dial a 1-800 number. There's great strength in having a group of talented people around you who are experts in various fields and who can help you solve problems you don't have the answers to on your own.

Each of us only has a finite amount of knowledge, but having these strong relationships allows us to overcome what we don't know. When you're spending less time and money on those tasks, you're able to spend more time and money on the things you want to be doing; the things that make you happy. Because we view this strength as especially crucial, I'm going to ask you to stop here for a second and closely consider the following questions:

- What relationships do I have in my life that I can build upon?
- What can I do to enhance my current relationships?

No one has all of the strengths we just discussed; nobody is perfect. But instead of focusing on your weaknesses or past mistakes, focus on what it is you're doing well as a starting point to developing a good plan for yourself. Identify and reinforce your strengths. You may not realize how big of a deal they are, but you should.

Then, where there are areas of weakness—let's say you're notorious for having high expenses—pinpoint some agreeable solutions. If a lot of money is being spent on dining out at fancy restaurants multiple times a week, try trimming it back to just one night a week. Or, if dining out a lot brings you the most joy in your personal life, look at your expenses and figure out another area you can cut back on that wouldn't bother you as much. There may be solutions if you look hard enough.

CLIENTS WHO'VE REALIZED THEIR STRENGTHS

We've seen many clients come through our door who were focused on their financial weaknesses and mistakes and ended up discovering several strengths that they used to bolster their financial plans.

LOW EXPENSES AND A STABLE INCOME

When Martin and Delia came to me, Martin was beating himself up over some missed opportunities in the past. He made a few investments that didn't work out and other investments that he felt he should have made but didn't. He was gripped by regret over his decisions and was fearful he had cost him and Delia a comfortable future.

But from a financial planning perspective, that wasn't the case. Martin and Delia were excellent at managing their expenses. They were good savers from early in their marriage, so we had plenty to work with from a planning standpoint. Buying an RV was on their list of "what-ifs." They had dreamed of visiting the state parks, but Martin felt that goal was out of reach because of his financial hiccups.

We addressed Martin's concerns by reinforcing his strengths, which he was having a hard time recognizing. Instead of focusing on specific investments and numbers, we took Martin and Delia through their journey: Martin and Delia both worked steady jobs, together they had built up their savings, and they had already paid for their children's college education. In other words, they were in great shape, but someone needed to point that out for Martin.

We caution clients not to let perfection get in the way of progress. Martin was fixated on that ideal future we discussed in Chapter 2. Sure, we all wish we would have invested in Apple or Amazon very early on, but that's not how life shakes out for most of us. Martin needed to know that what he and Delia did was even more important than striking gold: they lived within their means and prioritized educating their children. Getting our clients to a place of gratitude is essential for us. At Cedar Brook, we believe gratitude grounds you and allows you to see the future more holistically.

For Martin, we tried to shift his focus from his missed opportunities and past mistakes to his good habits and stability. We told Martin and Delia, "You're in a solid position. You've earned this, and you've done it together. You should be proud of what you built. Everything didn't work out perfectly for you, but it doesn't for anyone. You don't have to let that uncertainty dictate your future."

Martin and Delia worked with another advisor for a long time before they came to us, and that advisor's conventional wisdom and impersonal approach weren't effectively maximizing their resources. They needed something different to take their financial plan to the next level, but Martin was naturally skeptical. He'd seen things go wrong, so when he came to us, he wanted to know when the other shoe would drop. Delia, on the other hand, was ready. They worked hard to get to this point, and she wanted to enjoy the payoff for all their work. But Martin's fears were holding them back. That's why we were glad they came to Cedar Brook.

The moment it clicked for him was the preliminary financial

plan meeting. We call it "the Decision Center." Martin sat across from me and said, "All right, it sounds great in theory, but what are you missing? What if 'X' happens? What if 'Y' happens? What if the world implodes?" And we just modeled everything in. We just kept modeling every scenario he could come up with and said, "If 'X' happens, here's what it would look like, and here's how our plan will mitigate its impact on your future."

Step by step, we used the numbers to prove to Martin that his past actions were more positive than he imagined. Once we took the weight off his past, we got Martin excited about his bigger future. He could daydream about making work optional, being there for his future grandkids, and hitting the open road in his new RV.

That's when I saw his swagger and confidence come back. Delia was filled with gratitude. She said, "Martin, let's not waste time." They dropped their advisor as a result of this process, and they started working with us exclusively.

PENSIONS AND SUMMER JOBS

Isabel and Logan are two other clients who came to us with their financial weaknesses top of mind but realized they had plenty of strengths working in their favor. Isabel and Logan were both teachers and have pensions (huge win!). They've always been scrappers, and throughout their careers, they also kept jobs in the summertime. Not only were they always working, but they were diligent about keeping their expenses low, too.

These strengths resulted in good cash flow, and they bought a couple of rental properties as investments. They've since paid off the mortgages on those properties and now make a nice, steady income from them in retirement. Between that and their teacher pensions, all of their needs—and more—are covered.

Beyond all of that, they also have about $3 million saved from long-term compounding, and they don't touch that money simply because they don't need to. They consider that $3 million a legacy for their children, a rainy day fund in case of a health event, or for anything else unexpected that may arise. Despite having a substantial net worth, they still keep expenses low. They don't drive fancy cars, wear expensive clothes, or spend much on material things. Isabel and Logan live a simple, happy life.

For whatever reason—perhaps lack of confidence or modesty, as I've mentioned other clients get caught up in—when Isabel and Logan came to us, they thought they didn't have much; they found it hard to see their strengths. For example, they didn't consider how much value their pensions held. Once we could show them how many strengths existed, they could clearly see how much wiggle room they had. At that point, they started to feel confident that they could begin incorporating more travel into their lives and purchasing things they wanted, like new bikes, since they are avid cyclists. They had underestimated and discounted themselves, feeling like they were falling behind, but once they were aware and accepting of their strengths, they were able to begin doing and spending on the things they wanted.

HIGH-PAYING PROJECTS AND FLEXIBILITY

Another couple, Carlotta and Ronan, are a writer/director and an actor, respectively, in their mid-thirties. Carlotta has worked her way up the ladder in her field and is now on a very significant project with Disney. Both of them are creatives by nature, and numbers, in general, are confusing to them. Since they both work on a project-by-project basis in non-traditional jobs—feeling adrift from the rest of the world—they were scared they would have to work forever just to make ends meet. They were fearful they'd also need to rush from project to project to stay afloat. All in all, they were stressed.

We went through The Humanity Factor™ with them, focusing on their strengths, and were able to show them they had a lot more breathing room than they imagined. Although they were project-based, some projects paid a great deal of money and offered more flexibility to save in those moments. Carlotta's current project is high-paying but is also very time-consuming and detail-oriented. So Ronan elected to take a break from acting projects and teach acting for the time being so he can be home with their toddler-aged daughter. This saves them money in childcare, offers flexibility, and allows them to save more of the funds coming in from Carlotta's project.

We also showed them how the extra income from some of their projects could allow for free time in between to celebrate and breathe before they rushed off to their next gig. It gave them a lot of confidence and addressed the worry they may have otherwise carried with them for the next 30 years, constantly stressing whether they would financially make it or not. By getting them to focus on their strengths, we were able to ground them while unwrapping some of the mystery they'd previously felt around the numbers.

OUTLINE YOUR STRENGTHS—AND USE THEM!

I hope you're now starting to think about the good things you've been doing that will benefit your plan. By maximizing your strengths, you're going to be able to live the exact future you wish for yourself. No matter where you are right now, have some gratitude for your situation and take a moment to appreciate the hard work you've already done. You are so much further along than you think you are, and we'll use all your strengths to take you *even* further.

Now that you feel more confident in your past and future, we'll take advantage of your strengths, gifts, and resources as we outline your numbers. You're fully equipped to realize the future you want, so let's solve the high school math problem that is *your retirement.*

CHAPTER 6

Putting It Together

We've gotten to the core of what motivates you, determined how to address your fears, overcome weaknesses, and focused on your strengths. It's time to get to the numbers.

I've mentioned that Cedar Brook does not put numbers first, but we *do* care about the numbers. Everything we've covered so far has provided context so that the numbers will have real meaning for you as you begin to examine them. At this point, you should be clear on what you want for your future, and your numbers will dictate exactly how you can get there.

At a high level, what we'll do with our clients is look at their typical expenses and say, "If Chris and Rachel spend $100,000 a year, once you've deducted their income—Rachel's pension and their social security—how much more do they need to cover expenses?" Then, we estimate how long they'll live on that money so they have enough accumulated. We don't want clients finding themselves in their eighties without two pennies to pinch together.

Throughout this chapter, I'll show you the basics of a sample financial plan with the goal of helping you create a clear, manageable plan of your own—one that's grounded, personal, and within reach. I will thoroughly walk you through the sample documents so that you can apply them to get clear on your retirement readiness.

Even if you're not a numbers person, you should find this fairly simple. And once you've plugged some of your own numbers in, you'll likely find some of your fears addressed, too. Since now your numbers will be all about *you*, you'll likely find them more interesting, as they're directly linked to your opportunities and desires.

CREATING A FINANCIAL PLAN

The goal of developing a financial plan is to provide you with confidence and clarity about your bigger future, even when chaos reigns. The plan will help you move from where you are now to where you want to be. Putting together a financial plan that is unique to you will help you see your financial life in an organized and detailed scope.

WHAT DOES A FINANCIAL PLAN INCLUDE?

A financial plan addresses a myriad of concerns and goals, from managing your investments, including illiquid assets like concentrated stock positions or business ownership, estate planning, generating retirement income, and saving for college, to name a few. Depending on your needs, your plan may narrow in on one element or address multiple goals you'd like to achieve over time. Whatever you choose to focus on, your financial plan is designed to serve as your road map, helping you navigate the years before, during, and after your transition to retirement.

A good financial plan should give you a detailed, complete view of your current financial situation, thorough modeling of where you want to be, and the actions you need to take to reach those goals. It should address all the pieces of your financial puzzle, from stresses and fears to your values and dreams, and include risk factors, cash flow, retirement, estate planning, taxes, education, and income strategies to help bring you clarity and guidance. Through this planning process, we can help you prepare for life's expected *and* unexpected circumstances. Planning is a dynamic process, not a static one, because things change in our lives. The planning process creates a baseline we can work from as those changes arise. The result is a simple yet powerful road map to guide you toward financial freedom.

CEDAR BROOK'S SAMPLE DOCUMENTS

Cedar Brook developed three sample documents that are part of a good financial plan. These documents are all based on a fictional person's income plan and how we developed it, including identifying their goals, creating a balance sheet, reviewing their cash flow, and more.

I'm going to walk you through the following three samples:

- Living Plan Document
- Cash Flow Analysis
- Visual Cash Flow Analysis

Again, remember that these are only hypothetical plans and the characters and circumstances are completely fictional and for illustrative purposes only. Do not rely on any of the examples to make personal financial decisions. These samples will, however, give you an idea of how our process may help you accomplish your goals and enjoy financial freedom.

LIVING PLAN DOCUMENT

Your Living Plan Summary
Prepared for Mr. and Mrs. Client

Short-Term Goals/Cash Flow Needs

Objectives
- Allocate sufficient assets for the purchase of the home in Florida.

Assumptions
- The purchase price of the home in Florida is $390,000. You have made a $20,000 down payment and will pay the balance due of $370,000 prior to the end of the year.
- In addition to the funds needed to complete the purchase of this home, you want to account for additional living expenses of $25,000 per year, adjusted for inflation, beginning January of next year.

Observations & Recommendations
- As you will see in the cash flow projections, $370,000 is included as an expense line item. These funds will come from your money market account.
- The additional living expenses of $25,000 per year are also included as a line item in your cash flow beginning next year. These expenses will be adjusted for inflation.

Financial Independence

Objectives
- Ensure assets are sufficient in order to maintain your current standard of living during retirement and throughout your lifetimes.
- Coordinate retirement planning with investment planning.

Assumptions
- Both of you are retired.
- General Assumptions:
  - Inflation Rate: 2.44% based on the historical Consumer Price Index
  - Tax Rates: Federal calculated based on Form 1040; State based on OH
  - Growth Rates: Your blended rate of return is approx. 5%
  - Life Expectancy: Age 95

- Current income and expenses:
  - Based on the information provided, your current income is as follows:
    - Pension #1: $97,284 per year, no inflation
    - Pension #2: $5,980 per year, no inflation
    - Mr. Client's Social Security: $39,989 per year, inflating 1.5% annually
    - Mrs. Client's Social Security: $17,138 per year, inflating 1.5% annually

  - Based on the information provided, your current expenses are $180,000 per year, broken down as follows:
    - General Living Expenses: $155,494 per year, adjusted for inflation
    - Liabilities: $15,360 per year, level until paid off
    - Insurance Premiums: $9,146 per year, level

- In addition to the above expenses, we have included Medicare payments for supplemental coverage of $4,000 per year per person. These expenses will be adjusted for inflation.

- Future Income Sources:
    - Mr. Client's required minimum distributions (RMDs) will begin at age 72 in 2030.
    - Mrs. Client's RMDs will also begin at age 72, in 2031.

Observations & Recommendations

Based on the above assumptions, and an assumed rate of return of approx. 5% per year, you are well-positioned to withdraw the necessary funds from your portfolio to support your spending goals throughout your lifetimes. As you can see from the graph below, your net investable assets decrease slowly over your lifetimes, with a projected value of approx. $1.8 million at age 95.

End of Year Liquid Investable Assets From Current Age Until Death of Last Survivor

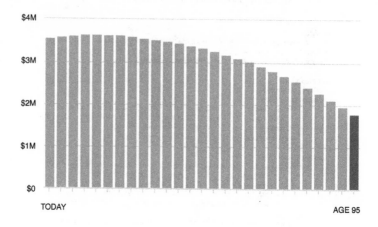

- Segmentation of Assets
  - o By taking a segmentation of assets approach to the portfolio, we are minimizing the overall volatility of the portfolio.
  - o With this approach, we break out your assets into "segments."
    - The first segment is typically funded with enough assets to support your income needs for the first 3 years of retirement. These assets are invested primarily in cash and cash equivalents and are "safe" monies that should not be affected by market downturns or adjustments. Often these funds are left in your bank accounts, such as your checking and money market accounts.
    - The second segment is funded with assets that will potentially grow for 3 years (while segment 1 is being spent) and will be sufficient to support the next 3–5 years of your retirement. Since the funds will still be needed in a relatively short period of time, they will be invested conservatively in short-term bond instruments, laddered CDs, or other cash-like alternatives. The target rate of return for these funds is typically about 3%.
    - The third segment will also be spent down over a 5–7 year period but will be invested for 6–8 years before funds are ever needed to support income needs. Therefore, this segment can typically be invested in balanced and growth and income assets. The target rate of return for these funds is approx. 4–5%.
    - The final segment is allocated for funds that will not be needed to support income needs for at least 15 years. These funds can withstand a little market volatility with time to recover over the 15 years in the event there is a market adjustment. In your case, there is not a need to take on unnecessary volatility to achieve a high rate of return since we've already demonstrated that your 3% rate of return can support your lifetime spending needs. But this last segment can be funded with assets that take on some volatility to get a slightly higher rate of return around 5–6%, allowing you to either increase your future spending goals or pass on more wealth to the next generation or leave a family legacy through your grandchildren or other charitable causes.

Your Living Plan Summary
Prepared for Mr. and Mrs. Client

Investment Planning

Objectives

- Review current investment portfolio for proper diversification and asset allocation.
- Implement an effective method for monitoring your investment portfolio and develop an income distribution strategy to meet your spending needs in retirement.

Assumptions

- A 5% gross annual rate of return is projected on net investable assets before and during your financial independence.

Observations & Recommendations

- Based on your current investment breakdown, your blended rate of return is 2.9%

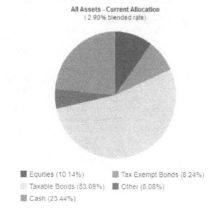

All Assets - Current Allocation
(2.90% blended rate)

- Equities (10.14%)
- Tax Exempt Bonds (8.24%)
- Taxable Bonds (53.09%)
- Other (5.08%)
- Cash (23.44%)

Your Living Plan Summary

Risk Management
Survivor Income Needs

Objectives
- Ensure assets are sufficient in order for the surviving spouse to maintain the current standard of living in the event of a premature death.
- Review portfolio of life insurance coverage to ensure it is appropriate for your needs and objectives.

Assumptions
- See *Life Insurance Summary* for details.

Observations & Recommendations
- Life Insurance Policy Analysis
  - ABC Insurance Company

Issue Date	March 2000
Current Death Benefit	$100,000
Net Surrender Value	$53,000
Cost Basis	$51,300
Policy Gain	$1,700
Monthly Premium	$213.76
Underwriting Class	Standard Smoker

    Options available:
    1. Keep As-Is
       - If Mr. Client continues to pay the premium on this policy, it is guaranteed to remain in force to age 100. The dividends received are currently being used to purchase paid-up additions. Therefore, the projected death benefit at age 80 is approx. $129,000, and the projected cash value at age 80 is approx. $96,000.
    2. Surrender Policy
       - Mr. Client has the option of cashing in the policy for the projected net surrender value of approx. $53,000. If he does this, there will be a small taxable gain to report of about $1,900. These funds could then be reinvested or used toward the purchase of your Florida home later this year.
    3. Reduced Paid-Up Policy
       - If Mr. Client no longer wishes to pay the premium to maintain the current death benefit, he has the option of taking a reduced paid-up policy. This would provide him a death benefit of approx. $80,200 that is guaranteed until age 100. No further premiums would be due. The projected death benefit at age 80 would be approx. $91,600, and the projected cash value at age 80 is approx. $74,000.

4. Cash Value Exchange to New Policy
   - Finally, Mr. Client could leverage the current cash value in the policy of approx. $53,000 and purchase a new policy. Because he is no longer a smoker, we are assuming an underwriting class of standard non-smoker. A new policy could potentially provide a death benefit of $100,000, which is guaranteed to age 121 with no further premiums due (compared to the $80,200 of the existing policy). The death benefit would remain at $100,000 at age 80, and the projected cash value is approx. $58,000 at age 80. This policy is designed to maintain the death benefit, not accumulate cash value.

- Policy Recommendations
  - As you can see, there are several options available to Mr. Client in regards to his ABC Life Insurance policy. We do not feel this death benefit is needed to create income for Mrs. Client in the event of his premature death. However, we do not believe it is in his best interest to surrender it for the cash value. You have more than sufficient cash and other liquid assets to complete the Florida home purchase, and you've invested in this policy for 20 years and can leverage the funds you have accumulated.

  - Because there may be a change in underwriting due to his non-smoker status, this is a good time to completely review all the options. Maintaining this death benefit will provide Mrs. Client with a lump sum of cash to cover final expenses and other expenditures in the event of his premature death.

Mrs. Client's Life Insurance Policy Analysis
- XYZ Life Insurance Company

Issue Date	September 1979
Current Death Benefit	$8,000
Cash Value	$5,000
Cost Basis	unknown
Quarterly Premium	$21.50
Underwriting Class	Smoker

Options available:
1. Keep As-Is
   - If Mrs. Client continues to pay the premium on this policy, it is projected to remain in force to age 100. The dividends received are currently being used to purchase paid-up additions. The projected death benefit at age 100 is approx. $7,500.

2. Stop Paying Premiums
   - If Mrs. Client stops paying the premium on this policy, it is still projected to remain in force to age 100. However, the projected death benefit at age 100 is approx. $4,500 since cash from the policy will be used to pay the premium.

3. Reduced Paid-Up Policy
   - Finally, Mrs. Client also has the option of electing a reduced paid-up policy with a reduced death benefit of approx. $7,300. This option would require no further out of pocket premiums nor any premiums from the cash value of the policy. The loan balance would also be paid off. This death benefit is projected to remain in force until age 100.

   o Policy Recommendations
   - As you can see, there are several options available to Mrs. Client in regards to her life insurance policy. Because of the size of the death benefit, we feel the best course of action for this policy is to take a reduced paid-up policy and keep it in force for her lifetime.

Long-Term Care

Objectives
Protect assets from depletion due to the need for in-home or long-term nursing care.

Assumptions
Both of you are insured in the event of a long-term care need.
See *Long-Term Care Insurance Summary* for details.

Observations & Recommendations
Long-term care planning is an important component of most people's overall financial plan, and you've taken the first important step by purchasing long-term care insurance coverage. We strongly recommend keeping this coverage in place by continuing to pay the premiums and will periodically review the policy to ensure it continues to remain cost efficient.

Since 2004, Genworth has uncovered several trends in the long-term care services landscape. Not surprisingly, the cost of all types of care has steadily risen over the years—from homemaker services to nursing home care. However, the cost of care provided in people's homes has not risen by the same degree as care provided in facilities. Genworth's experience shows that the majority of claims begin in the home. Both of your existing policies provide for a 100% of the nursing home facility benefit for services received in the home.

Estate Planning

Objectives

- Review current estate planning documents and ensure proper planning documents are in place.
- Provide ideas for a plan that offers flexibility.
- Implement strategies that will reduce future estate tax liability.
- Ensure assets are properly titled to attain your goals.

Assumptions

- We reviewed the following estate planning documents for Mr. and Mrs. Client:
  - Last Will and Testament
  - Durable Power of Attorney

Observations & Recommendations

- Current Documents
  - You recently had your wills and durable powers of attorney drafted and executed. There is not a need at this time to have these reviewed, but if you decide to move forward with a trust, it will be important to make sure the two documents are coordinated. It may be necessary to write a codicil to your will in order to ensure it coordinates with the trust. This can easily be done with your attorney.
  - In addition to your wills and powers of attorney, the following documents should be part of your overall estate plan:
    - Living Wills
      - A Living Will is a document that allows a person to explain in writing which medical treatment he or she does or does not want during a terminal illness. A Living Will takes effect only when the patient is incapacitated and can no longer express his or her wishes.

    - Healthcare Powers of Attorney
      - This document gives the person you designate (the attorney-in-fact) the power to make most healthcare decisions for you if you lose the capacity to make informed healthcare decisions for yourself.

Trust Planning

- **Protection & Control of Assets**
  - Would you prefer that your assets stay in your own family? *Without a proper plan*, your child's spouse may wind up with your money if your child passes away prematurely or gets divorced. Your current documents address the issue of a premature death as your assets will pass to a grandchild if his or her parent predeceases you. These assets passing to your grandchildren will be held in trust until age 30. However, if your child divorces his or her current spouse, your assets could end up inadvertently going to the former spouse. *With a plan*, you can set up a trust that ensures your assets will stay in your family, regardless of death or divorce.

- **Assets for Grandchildren**
  - A trust can also allow you to establish a special gift fund for each grandchild, if you so desire. You could designate a specific dollar amount that would pass in trust for their benefit to be given to them at a specific time in the future, such as when they get married, purchase their first home, or have their first baby. It could be a way to create a memorable gift for your loved ones.

Cedar Brook is a registered investment advisor. This is a hypothetical example for a general audience. This is a performance report depicting the performance results over a twenty-seven-year period. The material conditions, objectives, and investment strategies used to obtain these results were generated in eMoney financial planning software. The results are net of the management fees that are charged to clients of the firm. The results reflect the reinvestment of dividends or other earnings. Any hypothetical examples contained in this document are for illustrative purposes only. They do not represent the past or future portfolio composition or performance of any specific investment and are not intended as investment advice. We suggest working with your financial professional to see which allocation opportunities may be right for you.

In order to create a thorough Living Plan for clients, we first consider what was uncovered in the development of their Unique Story. This helps us identify their objective. You'll notice in this fictional example Mr. and Mrs. Client have an objective to purchase a vacation home in Florida. We assumed the purchase price in the neighborhood they wanted was $390,000. We noted that the couple has $20,000 to make a down payment, resulting in a mortgage of $370,000. Then, we factored in the additional living expenses needed, like property taxes, yard maintenance, electricity, water, and gas, among others. We assumed those additional living expenses would amount to about $25,000 per year.

Next, we discuss the clients' financial independence. Their objective here is to ensure they're able to sustain their lifestyle through the entirety of their retirement. Scoping this out allows us to tell the clients whether they're on track or not. To do this, we walk through some other assumptions with them—because the plan is only as good as what we put into it.

In this example, we assume Mr. and Mrs. Client are both retired. We also have to account here for inflation and grow expenses based on that percentage. We *also* make an assumption on taxes as well as one on growth rates, which in this case, we set at 5 percent for illustrative purposes.

Another assumption we also need to include here is how many years a person's retirement savings will need to last them. We set an "end date," or in other words, an estimate of how long the person/people believe they're going to live. This topic can be uncomfortable to discuss, but it's essential to estimate life expectancy if the client doesn't want to outlive their money.

We then move to some other basic assumptions, plugging in numbers for income, expenses, and future income sources. You'll see both Mr. and Mrs. Client have pensions, which is great. We've also included Social Security here as income, and in terms of expenses, we take it beyond typical living expenses and expand it to include things like liabilities and insurance premiums. It's important to get these numbers right because the accuracy of these numbers will determine if their objectives can be met without worry.

The next page of the Living Plan is the *grand reveal*. This is the moment where we're able to show Mr. and Mrs. Client that they are—in fact—on track, based on those numbers we just crunched, and that they can afford the Florida home. The numbers ultimately show us here that, at age ninety-five, when the second spouse dies, in this illustration, they would have $1.8 million left for their kids.

At this point, we'd begin to ask clients questions like, "Do you want to leave a legacy of $1.8 million for your kids? Or do you want to have some fun with some of the money *now* while you're alive?" It starts additional conversations about what they want to use their money for, knowing exactly what that dollar amount is, and realizing just how much flexibility they have.

We don't make decisions until we've also discussed risk management. This is where the segmentation of assets comes in because erratic market performance is something that can spoil a good plan. This section of the Living Plan focuses on how to get around worst-case scenarios—like if Mr. or Mrs. Client passes away sooner than expected and income decreases while expenses remain the same. In that case, what would happen to the money intended for their children? Estate planning is essential to a thorough financial plan because if someone passes away, it ensures the important assets will be distributed to the right people in the desired manner.

Risk management and debt retirement are not the most fun steps to walk through, but they're very practical in protecting your family if something unexpected happens. We plan for that as a means of cutting to the chase. We want to have thought through the most possible circumstances so that people can quickly and easily assess their situation and feel good about it. This is where the rubber meets the road.

CASH FLOW ANALYSIS

5-Year Cash Flow

Base Facts
Prepared for Mr. and Mrs. Client

The 5- Year Cash Flow report illustrates your income, savings, expenses, and resulting net cash flow on an annual basis.

Year/Age	2023 (65/66)	2024 (66/67)	2025 (67/68)	2026 (68/69)	2027 (69/70)
Portfolio Asset Balances (Beginning of Year)					
Taxable Investments	1,577,645	1,599,503	1,642,676	1,685,783	1,731,588
Retirement Accounts	1,545,576	1,537,387	1,531,229	1,522,849	1,512,348
Cash Accounts	693,403	708,266	698,283	687,683	657,884
Insurance Accounts	58,347	59,672	61,026	62,411	63,828
Total Portfolio Asset Balances (Beginning of Year)	**3,874,971**	**3,904,828**	**3,933,214**	**3,958,726**	**3,965,648**
Cash Inflows					
Social Security	59,984	60,884	61,797	62,724	63,665
Deferred Income					
Pension #1	97,284	97,284	97,284	97,284	97,284
Pension #2	5,980	5,980	5,980	5,980	5,980
Planned Distributions	60,301	58,012	60,045	61,902	63,810
Total Cash Inflows	**223,549**	**222,160**	**225,106**	**227,890**	**230,739**
Cash Outflows					
Living Expenses	155,494	159,024	162,634	166,326	170,102
Liabilities	15,360	15,360	15,360	15,360	15,360
Insurance Premiums	9,146	9,146	9,146	9,146	9,146
Taxes	30,272	30,306	31,103	47,167	47,482
Other Expenses					
Mrs. Client's Medicare Payment	4,000	4,091	4,184	4,279	4,376
Florida Home Expenses	25,000	25,568	26,148	26,742	27,349
Mr. Client's Medicare Payment	4,000	4,091	4,184	4,279	4,376
Total Cash Outflows	**243,272**	**247,586**	**252,759**	**273,299**	**278,191**
Total Inflows	**223,549**	**222,160**	**225,106**	**227,890**	**230,739**
LESS: Total Outflows	243,272	247,586	252,759	273,299	278,191
EQUALS: Net Cash Flow	**(19,723)**	**(25,426)**	**(27,653)**	**(45,409)**	**(47,452)**
Portfolio Growth	109,881	111,824	113,210	114,233	108,508
Other Portfolio Activity	(60,301)	(58,012)	(60,045)	(61,902)	(63,810)
Total Portfolio Asset Balances (End of Year)	**3,904,828**	**3,933,214**	**3,958,726**	**3,965,648**	**3,968,894**

This analysis must be reviewed in conjunction with the limitations and conditions disclosed in the Disclaimer page. Projections are based on assumptions provided by the advisor/representative, and are not guaranteed. Actual results will vary, perhaps to a significant degree. The projected reports are hypothetical in nature and for illustrative purposes only. Return assumptions do not reflect the deduction of any commissions. They will reflect any fees or product charges when entered by the advisor/ representative. Deduction of such charges would result in a lower rate of return. Consult your legal and/or tax advisor before implementing any tax or legal strategies.

Version 10.3.568.33903 § Prepared March 2021 by Cedar Brook Group §
Personal and Confidential §

5-Year Cash Flow

Base Facts
Prepared for Mr. and Mrs. Client

The 5- Year Cash Flow report illustrates your income, savings, expenses, and resulting net cash flow on an annual basis.

Year/Age	2028 (70/71)	2029 (71/72)	2030 (72/73)	2031 (73/74)	2032 (74/75)
Portfolio Asset Balances (Beginning of Year)					
Taxable Investments	1,778,650	1,827,005	1,876,688	1,927,734	1,980,185
Retirement Accounts	1,499,602	1,484,771	1,467,450	1,447,502	1,424,784
Cash Accounts	625,365	582,394	536,360	487,164	433,113
Insurance Accounts	65,277	66,759	68,275	69,825	71,410
Total Portfolio Asset Balances (Beginning of Year)	**3,968,894**	**3,960,929**	**3,948,773**	**3,932,225**	**3,909,492**
Cash Inflows					
Social Security	64,620	65,589	66,573	67,572	68,586
Deferred Income					
Pension #1	97,284	97,284	97,284	97,284	97,284
Pension #2	5,980	5,980	5,980	5,980	5,980
Planned Distributions	65,482	67,487	69,545	71,655	73,440
Total Cash Inflows	**233,366**	**236,340**	**239,382**	**242,491**	**245,290**
Cash Outflows					
Living Expenses	173,963	177,912	181,951	186,081	190,305
Liabilities	15,360	15,360	15,360	15,360	15,360
Insurance Premiums	9,146	9,146	9,146	9,146	9,146
Taxes	55,144	55,417	55,680	57,522	58,441
Other Expenses					
Mrs. Client's Medicare Payment	4,475	4,577	4,681	4,787	4,896
Florida Home Expenses	27,970	28,605	29,254	29,918	30,597
Mr. Client's Medicare Payment	4,475	4,577	4,681	4,787	4,896
Total Cash Outflows	**290,533**	**295,594**	**300,753**	**307,601**	**313,641**
Total Inflows	233,366	236,340	239,382	242,491	245,290
LESS: Total Outflows	290,533	295,594	300,753	307,601	313,641
EQUALS: Net Cash Flow	**(57,167)**	**(59,254)**	**(61,371)**	**(65,110)**	**(68,351)**
Portfolio Growth	114,684	114,585	114,368	114,032	113,528
Other Portfolio Activity	(65,482)	(67,487)	(69,545)	(71,655)	(73,440)
Total Portfolio Asset Balances (End of Year)	**3,960,929**	**3,948,773**	**3,932,225**	**3,909,492**	**3,881,229**

This analysis must be reviewed in conjunction with the limitations and conditions disclosed in the Disclaimer page. Projections are based on assumptions provided by the advisor/representative, and are not guaranteed. Actual results will vary, perhaps to a significant degree. The projected reports are hypothetical in nature and for illustrative purposes only. Return assumptions do not reflect the deduction of any commissions. They will reflect any fees or product charges when entered by the advisor/ representative. Deduction of such charges would result in a lower rate of return. Consult your legal and/or tax advisor before implementing any tax or legal strategies.

Version 10.3.568.33903 § Prepared March 2021 by Cedar Brook Group §
Personal and Confidential §

Cedar Brook is a registered investment advisor. This is a hypothetical example for a general audience. This is a performance report depicting the performance results over a twenty-seven-year period. The material conditions, objectives, and investment strategies used to obtain these results were generated in eMoney financial planning software. The results are net of the management fees that are charged to clients of the firm. The results reflect the reinvestment of dividends or other earnings. Any hypothetical examples contained in this document are for illustrative purposes only. They do not represent the past or future portfolio composition or performance of any specific investment and are not intended as investment advice. We suggest working with your financial professional to see which allocation opportunities may be right for you.

We use the Cash Flow Report to look at a client's numbers in further detail. In the sample here, you'll see this is a ten-year analysis, and it starts with Mr. and Mrs. Client's income and savings at the top and expenses below it—all line items with exact dollar amounts. The purpose of the Cash Flow Report is to show us what the gap between income and expenses is. Based on that difference, we can think about allocating money to their priorities.

In the sample Cash Flow Report, the top part shows Mr. and Mrs. Client's assets. You'll notice taxable investments, which would be things like brokerage accounts—stocks, mutual funds, and other dollars held in a non-retirement account. Then, retirement accounts are things like 401(k)s, 403(b)s, IRAs, Roth IRAs, and so on. Cash accounts are things like bank checking and savings. Insurance accounts could be annuity or life insurance policies with a cash value.

In the present situation, we estimate we will grow investments by 5 percent for illustrative purposes, so you will notice growth from year-to-year. For this couple, pensions and Social Security are the income, as well as planned distributions (money coming out of a retirement account for things like required minimum distributions). All of those are shown here as inflows.

The living expenses are things like groceries, cell phones, cars, insurance, and other things that are evergreen. The living expenses number grows each year, as indicated, because of inflation. Liabilities are their own category because they eventually end, so we don't include them forever. The insurance premiums in this example are static, and taxes are based on specific scenarios, depending on what Mr. and Mrs. Client will owe in federal and state taxes at current rates. Then, we have other expenses like their Medicare supplemental insurance payments, and we've factored in their Florida home expenses for their new house.

After detailing all of these numbers as such, we total them up. Inflows in the first year were $223,549, and outflows were $243,272. That means they have to reach into their pocket for $19,723 to cover their living expenses. When you compare that to the nearly $4 million they have in total assets, that's very doable. But as you can imagine, if Mr. and Mrs. Client only had total assets amounting to $200,000, that would be a problem. $20,000 a year would mean they would need to be making a little more than 11.15 percent on their returns every year just to stay even.

Again, it's a high school math problem, right? They have assets, we've estimated their growth at a 5 percent annual rate for illustrative purposes, and they have their income tallied. When we remove their expenses, we hope there's money available to cover them, which in this case, there is.

VISUAL CASH FLOW ANALYSIS

Cash Flow Analysis

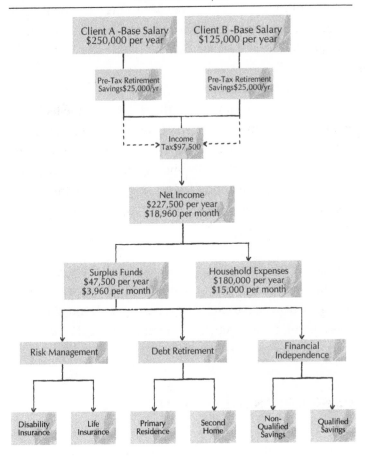

Cedar Brook Group

Cedar Brook is a registered investment advisor. This is a hypothetical example for a general audience. This is a performance report depicting the performance results over a twenty-seven-year period. The material conditions, objectives, and investment strategies used to obtain these results were generated in eMoney financial planning software. The results are net of the management fees that are charged to clients of the firm. The results reflect the reinvestment of dividends or other earnings. Any hypothetical examples contained in this document are for illustrative purposes only. They do not represent the past or future portfolio composition or performance of any specific investment and are not intended as investment advice. We suggest working with your financial professional to see which allocation opportunities may be right for you.

Finally, we put all of this into a visual representation for the clients. As you can see, this outlines the clients' numbers in a very easy-to-understand manner. While the ones you'll see in the sample here are not all of the elements we include for clients, they are the ones we see most often.

As you can tell, this is not pie-in-the-sky—this is tangible. And while we're not trying to teach the client all of the technical points when we put this together, we are holding their hand with their unique math problem. We like to show our work and prove to clients that their dreams are within reach. Once this is complete, they can more clearly see spots where they might need to revisit some of our earlier lessons, like planning for the unknowns, let's say.

More often than not, clients take a look at all three of the documents we just reviewed and are pleasantly surprised. Even in cases where unexpected things pop up in the numbers that cause alarm, going through the exercise—doing it now—gives the client time to course-correct.

USING A FINANCIAL PLAN IN REAL LIFE

As you're starting to look at your own numbers, you may see some things you can start doing today to improve your outlook and your chances for financial freedom in the future. The more time you have, the easier it will be to accomplish the goals. Even if things don't seem like they'll work out exactly the way you hoped, there is usually a way to make adjustments, pivot, and adapt.

This type of document lets you see everything happening with your finances, all in one place. This ensures that when you're adjusting things, you're doing so in the context of your greater plan instead of handling money in a silo without regard to how it impacts everything else. It also ensures you have continued options.

Let's put this in the context of the power couple Nick and Stephanie, who we discussed back in Chapter 2—the two executives in their mid-fifties who were looking to retire earlier than they originally planned. With financial independence as their most important objective, let's say they put all their numbers on the table and realize they can't quit their jobs as early as they'd like to. Looking closer at their numbers, we might say, "Alright, if you both want to retire earlier, would you be willing to work a stress-free job paying $30,000 a year for a couple of years instead of your current ones—whether it's consulting on the side or working at a local grocery store—we can make this work. What do you think?" We would discuss whether they think it would be worthwhile or not. Either way, this provides options and the clarity and confidence they need to make the right decision for them.

We have a client, Donald, who had his heart set on a very specific date for him and his wife, Janet, to both retire. They're both in their early sixties, and right now, he works for a manufacturing company, and she works at a school. Considering the state of the market, they didn't feel it was the right timing—they were fearful their numbers would find them white-knuckling it. For Donald and Janet, the most important objective in their Living Plan was to have a certain amount of extra pocket money during retirement. The way they saw it, they'd raised a family, always running a tight ship, and they'd worked really hard. But in retirement, they didn't want to have to live so tightly on cash; they wanted some extra wiggle room.

To make sure their retirement was as they envisioned, we crunched the numbers again, and they elected to work at least one more year—possibly two. They both like their jobs, so extending the date isn't a struggle. Now, they'll have less time they're living out of their portfolio and another year or two that they're saving. This means more money going into their growing pot.

Examining your numbers will allow you to make choices about your future instead of feeling like the money is in control of you. There's flexibility built into this for anyone. There's no one stringent way to go. There's more than one right answer; there are multiple right answers. When they're presented to you, you can decide how you want to make them as a family and do so confidently and without regret.

Planning ahead—and being mindful of the risk management portion of this—can prepare you for hard moments in your life. Consider a client of ours, Simone, who was married to an Army Ranger. He was involved in an off-duty boating accident and passed away, leaving behind Simone and three small children ages two, five, and seven. His family members' lives were instantly changed. At the time of her husband's passing, Simone was a stay-at-home mom. Luckily, her husband had life insurance, and she received benefits as a result of his military service as well. With that money, Simone was able to pay off their house. She then set some additional funding aside for the future and set some aside for tuition for herself to get her master's degree in counseling—pursuing a career that was of great interest and importance to her.

Because they'd planned ahead with life insurance, Simone was able to come out of the tragedy financially stable. Now, a few years later, her kids are all in school, and she has even more financial freedom to go on a summertime trip as a family or go camping with the kids. Despite the fact that her life is far different than she thought it was going to be, she is in a good place. In the years since her husband's passing, Simone has worked with us to create her own financial plan, and now she never has to live in fear that she won't be able to make things work. That clarity has relieved a lot of stress from her life, especially as someone who knows how quickly tides can change.

Having a clear financial plan allows you to really focus on the things that matter and not waste time worrying about the unknowns. By understanding the basic math, you can ensure you're not missing out on things you want to do just because you didn't know they were possible. A good financial plan helps you align your resources with your priorities, letting money be the tool to do the good stuff.

If something is possible, we encourage you to do it. Factor the numbers into your plan and make it happen. This entire exercise is about ensuring you can do the things you want to do confidently. And if things change along the way, you can rerun the numbers and quickly pivot—and do so as the central figure in your own planning.

CHAPTER 7

The Experience Index™

So, where are you right now in terms of planning for your future? We've covered a lot of information about The Humanity Factor™ approach. Still, if you're currently working with an advisor who doesn't see things the way we do, I recommend you uncover that sooner than later. To help with this, at Cedar Brook, we ask our clients to complete a questionnaire to benchmark their historic planning experience. We call that questionnaire The Experience Index™. In it, we include a range of questions that ground people and give them a sense of direction. The Experience Index is beneficial for clients who feel frustrated or lost regarding their current financial plan—or lack thereof.

By going through the questions in The Experience Index, clients can more easily find the path from a potentially hollow, numbers-centric plan to one that is truly humanity-driven. There's a higher correlation between taking a "humanity-driven" approach and achieving your financial goals than taking a "beat-the-markets" approach. In my opinion, focusing on performance alone actually *decreases* the likelihood of meeting your goals. We designed The Experience Index to help you shift your mindset from portfolio performance to personal experience.

TAKE THE EXPERIENCE INDEX

The Experience Index consists of twenty-six questions, most of which ask participants to read a statement and rate on a nine-point scale how strongly they believe or disagree with that statement.

You can also take the Experience Index online at https://franklegan.com/the-experience-index/

UNDERSTANDING YOUR RESULTS

This questionnaire proves helpful in gauging where you're at right now. The questions aim to bring about an understanding of these four categories as relevant to your unique financial plan:

- Clarity
- Relevance
- Alignment
- Leadership

Clarity scores you on whether or not you have a good focus on the people and things that matter most to you. Ideally, these questions will yield what's at the core of your decision-making.

If not, we put even more effort into that through The Humanity Factor approach.

Naturally, the people who score low with the Clarity questions tend to be more numbers-driven than anything else. They're the ones who walk into their bank and want to know the rate today—what they can get on a savings account or a CD. They don't tend to concern themselves with the *why* behind the dollars. Those who score higher with the Clarity questions are more in tune with their "why" and are more likely to share their "why" with their advisor.

Relevance scores you on how clearly your existing plan articulates the things that are important to you; it's all there in writing, in black and white. Low scores in Relevance are usually the result of vague plans, and high scores appear in Relevance when your plan is detailed and everyone in the room knows how vital your written objectives are for you. A good advisor will help you work toward those objectives all year long.

Alignment scores you on your conversations with your advisor and if they align with your values. It assumes the solutions you're implementing in your plan correlate with specific priorities. A high score indicates a strong connection between the plan you've built with your advisor and the life you want to lead.

Leadership considers your leader in this process—whether your advisor is thinking about you and your plan when you're not together and whether they're finding ways to add value for you and your family. This is our goal at Cedar Brook for our partners, associates and external collaborators. We do this by getting together internally to discuss the evolving financial landscape, including conversations about tax law changes, estate planning updates, and the investing landscape, to name a few. We also have a Future Look Committee that anticipates changes to how we deliver planning, considers potential challenges our clients will face, and examines macro trends happening in the economy. We bring what we know and share ideas and strategies as a group. We talk about both the big picture and our specific cases and clients. If one of our advisors gets stuck and is looking for another set of eyes on things, we jump in to help.

We see a lot of the same obstacles with clients day in and day out. Often, our clients have a degree of wealth that has created some level of complexity for them. Internally, we share with each other how to address these similar concerns cohesively. We do this at our biweekly meetings, for one. We also greatly benefit from our Wisdom Wednesdays since those discussions are also really robust and fun. It's nice to have the ability to walk down the hall, peek into somebody's office, and ask them for help in person. We have a spirit of cooperation and collaboration that exists here, and it enhances the experience for our clients tenfold.

This is just one of the ways to show leadership. It is our belief that whoever you're working with should exhibit strong leadership that yields positive, aligned results for you as their client. Be discerning about the kind of leader you want to take you through this process.

SEVEN INSPIRED QUESTIONS JOURNAL EXERCISE

Those taking The Experience Index can go through the questions online and then receive a follow-up email with their results.

This is also when we share some additional exercises with our clients that they can do to enhance their planning experience even further. We recommend clients print the exercises and record their thoughts long-hand instead of digitally because we find this tends to be more impactful.

First is our Seven Inspired Questions journal exercise. The Seven Inspired Questions allows clients to detail what's most important to them, why those things are important, and how to make sure everything in their plan is aligned with those very things. This helps clients find a sense of clarity while making sure we also have a continued understanding of how to best address their needs as we're contemplating their issues. As with many other aspects of The Humanity Factor, this helps ensure the client can continue doing the things they love most with the people they love most.

Going through these questions helps people see how their hard work and sacrifices—the things they do in their daily life—are of value. It serves as a great starting point for them to create a plan or a strategy around the most important elements in their life. In other words, it helps provide even greater alignment.

To our surprise, we discovered this exercise elicited heartwarming, emotional memories from our clients. The journal became not just a means to achieve alignment but also a space for reflection. We're human beings, we're emotional by nature, and so we need to make emotions a part of the planning process. When you invite emotion, you can harness it for good rather than denying it and having it drive you subconsciously.

The journal has become such a good communication tool and

touchpoint that our clients find it an enriching exercise to go through with their spouses. Although we recommend couples fill out the journal exercise separately, it helps them be fully candid about what they envision their ideal future to be like and how to get there.

The journaling exercise proves very motivating because it gets you to dream about what you want for your bigger future. As you're filling it out, you're examining your past, seeing how far you've come, and acknowledging the people that have been a part of getting you there. You'll notice, too, that it encourages you to focus on Mining Your Bliss, Cultivating Your Contributions, and The Leadership Lever, as we did in Chapter 2.

We've been using this exercise for many years, and we receive excellent feedback on it. It shows our clients where their satisfactions lie and reminds them they're a part of something bigger than themselves. It proves to be a better, less mundane approach than just focusing on the numbers. This becomes especially true when the clients begin sharing what's in their journals with us. Most people have never had conversations like these with their advisors—ones that force them to dig deep and make decisions about money based on the people and things that are important to them. Each time we have a conversation like this, it creates professional intimacy.

THE SEVEN INSPIRED QUESTIONS

1. Who matters most? Consider your most cherished relationships and document *who* matters most. Using the words below to stimulate your thinking, select your top five.

- Husband/wife/significant other
- Kids
- Grandkids
- Mother/father
- Siblings
- Other relatives
- Non-bloodline family/chosen family
- Friends
- Mentors
- Mentees
- People I work with
- People I play with
- Organizations (faith, health, purpose)
- Communities (geography, sports, faith)
- Other

2. What matters most? Consider *what* matters most for you personally and on behalf of the relationships you noted in Question #1. Using the words below to stimulate your thinking, select your top five.

- Physical health
- Faith/spirituality
- Emotional/mental health
- Financial success at work
- Financial success outside of work
- Physical fitness
- Safety
- Protection
- Education
- Hobbies
- Travel

- Advancement and growth
- Other

3. Why do they matter most? Consider *why* the people and topics you identified rose to your top three. Using the words below to stimulate your thinking, select your top five.

- Demonstrate love
- Offer compassion
- Pass on what's important
- Impact that outlives me
- Contentment for self and others
- Happiness/fulfillment for self and others
- Make the world a better place
- Lift up others
- Be a part of something bigger than myself
- Become better together
- Strengthen our communities (family, geography, faith, sports)
- Other

4. If you could eliminate the stress or distractions you experience around your financial affairs, what would you leave behind?

5. If you had time and resources to do the things you've always wanted to do with the people you cherish most, what might you envision?

6. Once you reduce your stress around financial affairs, how would you redirect the energy and mindshare that stress currently occupies?

7. Consider the top three areas for which increased clarity would allow you to feel more relaxed and joyful about your future and your family's future.

You can also print out our journal to answer these questions, which are listed below, or use your own.

Inspired Questions Weblink:

https://franklegan.com/IQ/

Journal Weblink:

www.franklegan.com/Journal

THE IMPORTANCE OF PROFESSIONAL INTIMACY

As clients go through their Seven Inspired Questions, we encourage them to be vulnerable. As with other parts of The Humanity Factor, a willingness to be honest and authentic will set you far ahead. It will help you get to the good stuff.

From an advisor standpoint, a client's vulnerability benefits us as well. It's our job to do the best we can for you and to help you plan for the future in the most effective way possible. Once the journal is complete, we encourage clients to share their sentiments with us. Because if we don't know them, we can't help them. The relationship becomes much stronger when you're willing to be sincere. The relationship becomes deeper instead of one that's simply transactional. Our clients are like family and friends to us.

Sometimes being honest about what you want can be scary because what if you can't get it? Or what if you don't deserve it? Or what if it's too much to even hope for? We remind clients here that you can't get something if you don't at least put it out there.

The result is professional intimacy. Sometimes, we find that our clients end up sharing things with us that they're not even comfortable telling the closest people in their lives. People share their deepest fears and their greatest hopes. We make sure they know what they're sharing with us doesn't go in one ear and out the other. It's what we call "living it versus learning it." We want to live it with our clients every day. There's a lot of trust-building that comes in here, and I can't stress this enough—your advisor should be someone you trust.

ON THE LEADING EDGE OF A NEW APPROACH

We designed the Humanity-driven Planning Continuum[8] (shown in the following image) to give you a sense of where the financial industry started, where it is now, and where the advisors at Cedar Brook would like it to go. It's helpful to consider how the industry has evolved when thinking about how to best work with a financial advisor.

The Humanity-Driven Planning Continuum
A New Way Forward

In the beginning, financial services companies were product-driven and transaction-based: if they sold something, they made money. In some cases, the product was a hammer and the client a nail, whether that product worked for the client or not.

Over time, financial firms had a second evolution: they wanted to smooth out their revenue and increase their objectivity so they didn't have to rely on selling products. That's when firms started charging ongoing management fees instead of commissions. This way, the advisor was able to make recommendations for the client without the client worrying that advice was based on them earning a commission instead of doing what was right.

---

8   Designed in collaboration with Jennifer Tolman of Second Summer, https://secondsummer.net.

The third evolution was a team-based approach where everybody has an area of expertise. This, in part, was designed to elevate the client experience. This approach broadened the technical solutions offered to clients. If you're just meeting a client once a year and changing one thing about their portfolio during that time, they start to wonder—is this service really worth what I'm paying?

Adding value for clients has been an important part of the financial planning model. And that's where Cedar Brook has come in and identified a fourth evolution: the human aspect.

Of course, as a company, we draw wisdom from the whole continuum, but we're taking it one step further—an important step. We're making each client the central figure in their own planning. As you go through the chapters and exercises in this book, you'll see that there's no such thing as one-size-fits-all when it comes to creating a good financial plan.

Cedar Brook is at the front of that curve, but not all firms are. This is a good time for you to take a look at your advisor and see where they fall. Are you working with someone who is on the front end of that curve or the back end? Remember, why not benchmark your experience with your existing advisor instead of benchmarking your performance? It will allow you to look back historically at what your experience has been and see whether you're in alignment.

Lots of firms are evolving. Make sure you're working with one of those firms. For us, we're really latched onto this humanity-driven concept because it has meaning behind it, and that makes our work even more fulfilling—and vital.

KEEPING A HUMAN APPROACH

The Experience Index is a helpful benchmarking tool that allows you to measure what your experience has been and whether you're in alignment with your goals and values or not. In the investment business, it's very common to compare performance to benchmarks. Through The Experience Index, we take that to the next level—beyond how your performance is doing against some arbitrary index, and rather we make it more meaningful to you and your experiences. It makes this process humanity-centric.

If you go through The Experience Index and don't feel great about your scores, allow this to be your catalyst to shop around for a new advisor. Comparison-shop with the realization that no two advisors are alike. There may be similarities, but they won't be exactly the same—not every advisor will care as much about the human aspect of your plan. There will always be other ways of going about things and other styles, and some will be a better match for you than others. Allow The Experience Index to serve as a filter to ensure you're working with the right people—those you're a good fit with. Because working with the wrong advisor can not only be ineffective, it can be an unnecessarily grueling process (and a waste of money!).

On our end, too, we know not every person would make the right client for Cedar Brook. Just as it's important for a prospective client to find the right advisor, it's important for us to find the right clients. More business doesn't mean anything to us if we're dissatisfied with our client-partner relationships. Make sure you choose an advisor with whom you have a Shared Purpose® relationship. You should both be excited about your meetings, and everyone should find it to be a rewarding process.

The best advisors will be happy to be invited on the journey with you.

Don't settle for a planning experience that is simply a transactional relationship. Benchmark your current experience (rather than assets or rates of return) and make necessary changes as needed to get you where you want to go.

Conclusion

Back in the Introduction, I challenged you to ask yourself this important question: do I believe my future is bigger than my past? If you didn't say *yes,* then I hope The Humanity Factor™ approach has helped change your mind. Believing that you can fulfill your dreams—and keeping the focus there—is fundamental to the process.

We've witnessed so many lightbulb moments with the people who have come through Cedar Brook's doors. We have watched with pride as our clients' mindsets shifted away from conventional wisdom—worrying about what everyone around them was doing and how they compared—to focus on *their* future and what would truly make them happy.

MARIA FULFILLS A POST-RETIREMENT DREAM

Maria is one of those clients. She came to us over a decade ago, a divorcee who'd been on her own for a while. She'd been able to remain financially stable for herself and her children and made some really good decisions to set them up for continued financial success. But she didn't always see it that way. Maria had trouble looking toward the future, but we pressed her and have continued to encourage her along the way using The Humanity Factor. Because of that, she's become hyper-focused on a future that would make *her* happy and has been willing to pivot her plan to bring those things to fruition consistently.

About a year ago—retired and in her seventies—Maria decided to follow her heart. Maria lives in Cleveland, but her daughter moved to Boston. As a result, Maria hadn't been able to spend as much time with her. She came up with the goal of selling her house in Cleveland and renting an apartment in a vibrant part of Boston close to her daughter. She knew she'd eventually aim to buy a place in the Boston area and settle down again, but she wanted to rent there for a year or two in the interim.

When Maria presented us with this goal, she had some worries, including being able to apartment-hunt while still in Cleveland and other logistics. She also worried, like so many do, whether she'd have enough money to make it all happen and how it would impact her finances down the road. So, we did what we like to do—we showed her our work. We showed Maria she had the opportunity to move states and still enjoy retirement with confidence. Once we relieved her concerns, we encouraged her to go for it. By freeing up her mental space from worrying about money, we left extra time for her to be excited and happy about the decision. Then, we were collectively able to celebrate.

I'm proud of Maria, and it's been great to see how happy she's been about this change. It put a pep in her step. She's more alive now than ever. The Humanity Factor approach allowed her to do this because it helped her reflect on her bigger future and reflect on the things that were most important to her, in this case, proximity to her family above all else.

If Maria had instead been focused on what other people her age were doing—and comparing herself to them—it's likely she would have never followed through on this goal, and there would have been some level of disappointment in not pursuing it. Instead, her plan helped her realize this goal with confidence, knowing that it wasn't going to hurt future Maria in any way. This hadn't been a part of her original plan for herself and her family, but it just goes to show how people's plans evolve over time. The Humanity Factor helped her make her ongoing dreams a reality.

Like the many other clients I've told you about in this book, Maria found The Humanity Factor approach comforting. She used this approach to her advantage, and I hope you will too. Like Maria, I hope that going through The Humanity Factor process and applying it to your financial future helps you get past the confusion, fear, and anxiety around financial planning and, in turn, helps you focus on your strengths, desires, and what matters most. By removing yourself from the rat race— leaving behind any tendency to compare yourself to what others are doing—you can best execute your personal goals, resulting in more successful financial outcomes.

I'm excited to have been able to share The Humanity Factor with you, as we've done with many clients over the years. Lots of them deal with fairly similar issues, and we provide them with tried and tested solutions, which is one of the reasons we wanted to put together this book. We use this strategy with every client, so we figured—why not share it with a bigger audience? So many people are going through the same worries and challenges, and their solution very well may be The Humanity Factor.

THE HUMANITY FACTOR, IN BRIEF

Before I leave you to it, I thought we'd quickly recap the key takeaways from each chapter's lesson.

CHAPTER 1 - THE HUMANITY FACTOR™

Our earliest discussions on The Humanity Factor encouraged you to start shifting your perception of financial planning away from conventional wisdom—a mentality of keeping up with the Joneses and one where it is *all* about the numbers—to a more human-centric mentality. Conversations that are numbers-only are hollow, at best. To truly create the best financial plan, you need to do some soul-searching to determine who you are, what's most important to you, and why it's important.

CHAPTER 2 - YOUR UNIQUE STORY

Developing your Unique Story is a step in the process that allows you to bring who you are and what you want into the equation of your broader plan. This part of The Humanity Factor framework calls on you to find gratitude when thinking about your past (acknowledging everything you've already accomplished), your present (taking stock of where you are currently), and your future (making plans that align with your biggest dreams). The development of your Unique Story helps you measure the *right* way instead of measuring against an ideal.

CHAPTER 3 - TRANSFORMING DANGERS

Transforming dangers is about the fear of losing something. It's all about pinpointing what unknowns scare you most about your financial future and planning for them ahead of time. This part of the process helps negate your "middle of the night" issues. It calls on you to understand the obstacles you could potentially face and develop a plan on how to jump over them before they ever become an obstacle. With those fears addressed and planned for, it helps lead to the *good stuff.*

CHAPTER 4 - MAXIMIZING OPPORTUNITY

Maximizing opportunities is about the excitement of gaining something. It challenges you to find an answer to this: when all is said and done, how do you want to spend your time, and with whom? Maximizing opportunities calls on you to dream bigger and bigger as you go along your journey. It goes hand-in-hand with transforming dangers because it's only once you've addressed your fears head-on that you can fully consider what's possible to achieve.

CHAPTER 5 - REINFORCING STRENGTHS

Right now, you're probably doing better than you think you are, but chances are you're not giving yourself credit. By being honest with yourself about the strengths you have, you can start to examine what you have working in your financial favor. It's important to take the things you're doing well... and maximize them!

CHAPTER 6 - PUTTING IT TOGETHER

This is where the numbers come in. Here, you're able to put

together a financial plan for yourself that capitalizes on your strengths, addresses your concerns, and focuses on what you care about most. Putting together a plan for yourself is where all of the previous lessons become tangible. It's where you're able to look at your numbers and see that you're OK after all. It's where you can see what's possible and where you can really start to have some fun.

CHAPTER 7 - THE EXPERIENCE INDEX™

The Experience Index™ is your benchmarking tool—a questionnaire that helps you understand what your planning experience is like right now and whether it's one you're content with or it's one that you can improve on, either with your existing advisor relationship or a new advisor. It helps you think through your *experience* as opposed to what your numbers alone are doing.

As you're continuing to apply The Humanity Factor, remember that addressing the unknown obstacles and fears can be scary, but so can being honest about what you want in life. Sometimes that part can be even scarier. Getting your hopes up, only to be let down, can deter people from getting real about their dreams. But you cannot achieve anything if you don't define it and work toward it. Really, what do you have to lose? You can't achieve your goals if you don't at least put them out there.

As you've gone through these lessons, I hope a light bulb went off for you, too, if you hadn't gotten it right away. Now that you're on the other side, I hope you've gotten to a place where you can begin feeling more vulnerable and honest about your dreams for the future, as well as your hopes for your family.

SURROUNDING YOURSELF WITH A GREAT TEAM

As I've mentioned, as you're going through the process of finding an advisor to help you, focus on seeking out one who has *you* in mind. There should also be a spirit of collaboration. As you've gathered, Cedar Brook takes this very seriously. That's why we're dedicated to having the right team in place to assist our clients. To do this, we have a rather tough interview process—one that ensures those we're hiring have the same collaborative spirit we do. We do this because we want to get it right for our clients. We're aware that one bad apple can spoil the batch. And we don't want that.

To best serve our clients, we rely on a business strategy of careful, intentional growth. As a result, we're able to maintain a laser focus on the expertise and resources that apply to each client's individual needs. It allows us to make a better plan, solve future problems, and identify bigger opportunities.

I use a system called Kolbe to measure a candidate's conative strengths in order to help us have the most well-rounded team. Kolbe helps us understand things like, if someone had twenty-four hours to themselves, how would they spend that time; what would they naturally gravitate toward doing?[9] Kolbe helps us as employers to build a team with Unique Abilities™.[10] This is important because, while certain tasks may seem to suck the life out of a person (perhaps because they're not good at them, or they are, but they just don't like doing them), that very task may be something a different person thoroughly enjoys spending time on and is good at.

---

9   Check out https://kolbe.com/ for help with how to define their system.

10   Sullivan, Dan, https://www.strategiccoach.com/.

Having our team scored by Kolbe helps us realize our ideal work day most of the time. Plus, you can imagine how much this benefits the clients, having our people internally playing to their strengths, doing the things they do best—the things that *give* them energy as opposed to things that *take* energy from them. When you're working in an environment like that, leading with The Humanity Factor™ approach becomes easier, in the sense that employees are happier and not feeling bogged down by clients (in fact, it's the opposite—they're enthused by the client's work).

Of course, this way of hiring makes sense, but not all work-places—especially financial firms—do that. For us, we simply do our best work that way. At Cedar Brook, we are not just a bunch of employees trying to make a living. We are, instead, putting it all out there for clients and living our own lives in parallel to our clients in many ways. Using Shared Purpose® as a compass, we experience a sense of gratitude that "flows in both directions." From us to our clients and back again. We care about each other beyond the business at hand. That's how we've developed this beautiful culture that we cherish. From the very early days, we knew we had something special with this approach, well before we even named it The Humanity Factor. We continue to be proud of it every day.

The Bliss Board is an exercise we did as a firm where everyone wrote down what they were grateful for. It's part of our values to live the work. We make sure to acknowledge what we're grate-ful for at Cedar Brook on a regular basis. I wanted to share it because it gives you a bit of insight into how The Humanity Factor impacts you when you apply these principles to your life and work.

To view the complete Bliss Board, scan the following QR code or go to www.franklegan.com/bliss-boards.

For my team, our core value is to put clients first in everything we do. We like to look at things through that lens. We also want to be optimistic, positive, and passionate about the work and have a tenacious, can-do attitude. We want to be holistic—looking at the whole person—and thorough, organized, proactive, helpful, and collaborative. We're not waiting for our clients to call us, we're out there trying to make things happen on their behalf, even when we're not together.

We want to be genuine, honest, and to do the right thing. We developed this ethos in order to have a clear purpose as a team internally so that clients could have a clear focus when they work with us as well. We *need* to all be on the same page. That is now part of our culture—in fact, it always has been.

As our next phase of bonding with clients, Cedar Brook is also working to become a bigger part of our community because we want to have influence beyond our business. We have a vision we're now working toward where we create communities for ourselves and clients to come together and volunteer. We plan to determine our volunteer opportunities based on things we know our clients feel most passionate about. For instance, if a health crisis has touched a client's life in some way, resulting in an interest in a supporting non-profit, we want to help them raise money and awareness for it. For example, Cedar Brook recently engaged in a Day of Service to honor one of our partners who lost their seven-year-old grandson in a car accident. It's vital that we support charities and causes that mean the most to our clients because our clients mean the most to us.

FINDING THE RIGHT FIRM

When seeking the right firm for you, I encourage one that's dedicated to developing professional intimacy—this is something so important to finding the right match. That professional intimacy helps develop bonding moments where you can get truly vulnerable and allow your advisor to be vulnerable with you, too. If you secure an advisor who puts you as the central figure in your own planning, together, you may achieve unprecedented results.

For me to further develop that professional intimacy, I time block an hour per week to write notes to clients—whether it's to celebrate something good that's happened in their life or to let them know we're thinking about them because they're going through a challenge. Clients really appreciate it, and it furthers our family-type bond.

It's also important that you keep the right team around you beyond your financial advisor. Planning for the future should not be done in silos since it requires experts in different areas. A great team is necessary for holistic success. We tell our potential new clients that, even if they have an existing team of experts around them, we aim to work alongside those experts seamlessly. If you work with us, it doesn't mean you need a new accountant or a new attorney or that you need to overhaul any of the existing relationships you have. We just become a part of the whole picture for you instead. That's how all advisors should view this.

Ultimately, I want to remind you to forget about the numbers; forget all the strategies, and focus on being happy first and foremost. I hope you will begin *living with* The Humanity Factor instead of just *learning* it. If finance seemed like a foreign language at the start, I hope you're now feeling comfortable enough to speak it. When you begin living with the positive results of The Humanity Factor, it becomes a part of you. I hope that is the case for you and that from here on out, you use this approach to live more intentionally and align your purpose in everything you do.

If you're interested in working with Cedar Brook Group, please find us on the web at franklegan.com and cedarbrookfinancial. com.

Acknowledgments

Thanks be to God.

Thanks to:

Laura and Reese for your enthusiastic support. Every day with you is a gift.

Mom and Dad for your love and understanding.

Jeff, Jill, Kelly, Sal, Grace, Claire, Maddie, Lil, and Salvatore. A big part of Our Humanity Factor.

Dale and Frank Diorio for all of your support.

Our clients, who inspire us to do our best work every day. Special thanks to those whose stories we share here.

Cedar Brook Family, it's an honor to do what we do together. Much respect and admiration for your many gifts.

Luci Charnas, Laurie Haynes, Dayna Smith, and Michael DeJohn, each day is a pleasure working alongside you.

Cedar Brook Humanity Factor Ambassadors, Bill Glubiak, April Menary, Dave Robertson, Laurel Caraboolad-Goldberg, Erin Stevenson, Christine Sivak, and Eve Hjort. Let's have dinner again soon.

Strategic Coach Dan Sullivan, Babs Smith, Adrienne Duffy, Kim Butler, Stephanie Song, and Kayanne Ratay, among so many others. Coach has been a transformative experience in my life. Thank you for challenging us to think about our thinking and for your unending support and enthusiasm. See you next quarter.

Jennifer Summer Tolman for encouraging us to live it and to be vulnerable.

Anne Sobel, the most amazing Scribe imaginable. It was so much fun working with you. I miss our Thursday mornings.

Darnah Mercieca, my favorite Author Success Manager. Thank you for skillfully guiding me through this process.

Scribe Media Team. The best in the business.

Howard Grossman for the amazing cover designs.

Our partners and friends at Frontier Asset Management, led by Rob Miller, Geremy van Arkel, Gary Miller, and so many others, who allow us to spend more time with our clients and to think big on their behalf. Love and respect for your cowboy ethics.

Claire Akin, Chelsea Espe, and everyone at Indigo Marketing Agency. We are so happy we found you.

Jason Koblin at MechaDigital for helping us tell our story and for being so patient with us.

To our tax and legal friends who keep us up to date on all we need to know, Alyson Pattie, F. Eric Jochum, Dana DeCapite, Paul Valencic, and Bill Pattie.

The "Dudes" text chain, Michael Carin (MC), Alex Slemc, Ross DeJohn III (Triple Crown Winner), Brent Kaniecki (Total Package), Jeff Legan, Ross DeJohn Jr., Roger Morrison, Mark DeJohn, and Mike Kovacs ('22 League Champion) who provided much-needed levity and laughs throughout this process.

A special thanks to Charlie, my best four-legged friend. We love you, buddy.